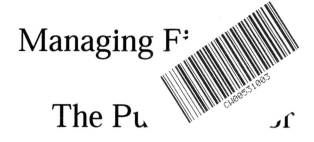

Managing F

The Pu   or

Managing For Servi   xcellence

By

William D. Brady, Jr., MA, CPPO

Managing Fixed Assets In The Public Sector

Copyright @ 2001 by William D. Brady, Jr
All right reserved

Universal Publishers / uPUBLISH.com
USA · 2001

ISBN: 1-58112-684-0

www.upublish.com/books/brady.htm

Introduction

The purpose of this text is to define and encourage conversation among public fixed assets management functions. No two-fixed assets management functions are alike. However, all share the same approaches in managing assets in their charge. I will attempt to define some key settings in managing fixed assets from defining fixed assets to accountability for those assets. This text was written to help better operate the day-to-day affairs of the public sector fixed assets management function. The information presented here is not new; however, the information is not contained in one concise location.

Additionally, it is my intention to stimulate conversation and communication on the subject of personal property management. In so doing, the expectation is that these conversations and communications will increase the effectiveness and efficiency of personal property management. The public sector is an area that relies on sound management practices and the management on those assets entrusted to us is no exception.

William D. Brady, Jr., MA, CPPO

Dedication

To my wife, Yolanda, who has inspired and supported me in all of my endeavors. Without her support I could not have accomplished this book or any of my other many endeavors.

Appreciation

I extend my sincere thanks to Mr. Richard Hamilton, Property Manger, The Citadel, Charleston, SC for his assistance. His assistance and counsel were invaluable in the preparation of this book.

The Author

William D. Brady, Jr., has served as the Director of Procurement Services at The Citadel, the Military College of South Carolina, in Charleston, South Carolina since 1987. He began has public purchasing career in 1983 after serving for 23 years with the United States Air Force. His duties include responsibilities for purchasing, supply management, fixed asset management and copier services. In 1987, he began service as a member of the Financial Records System (FRS) Team; a team designated to implement an automated financial system including a purchasing system. Since its formulation in 1987 the team has been responsible for implementation of the FRS Purchasing Module in 1990 and the Fixed Assets Module in 1991. He has attended ten of the past twelve annual International FRS conferences where he introduced presenters, served as a panelist for FRS purchasing and FOCUS topics and presented or hosted sessions on purchasing and fixed assets related topics. Mr. Brady has served as the President, Vice President, Program Committee Chairperson, and the Professional Development Chairperson of the South Carolina Association of Governmental Purchasing Officials (SCAGPO). The National Institute of Governmental Purchasing, Inc. (NIGP) selected him to be one of fourteen Procurement Management Auditors in 1996. Since then he has participated as a consultant in three audits, two for the District of Columbia and one for the University of the District of Columbia. Additionally, in 1998, he served as a member of the NIGP Ethics Committee, Education and Professional Development Committee, and the Procurement Procedures and Research Committee. In 1999, he served as the Vice-Chairperson of the NIGP Education and Professional Development Committee. The NIGP Technical Bulletin has published two of his articles related to public purchasing. He is a NIGP Master Instructor and an Associate Professor for Embry-Riddle Aeronautical

University. For NIGP, he teaches General Public Purchasing, Intermediate Public Purchasing, Electronic Purchasing, Contracting Out for Services, Specification Writing and Inventory and Warehouse Management. With Embry-Riddle Aeronautical University, he teaches graduate courses in business and management. A graduate of Washburn University with a Bachelor of Business Administration degree, he has a Master of Arts degree in management and supervision from Central Michigan University. His professional certification is as a Certified Public Purchasing Officer (CPPO).

Table of Contents

List of Figures

List of Tables

Chapter 1 Introduction

Purpose

The primary purpose of this chapter is to introduce the field of fixed assets management. It describes the nature and scope of fixed assets management and how it relates to the other segments of the public agency.

Objectives

Upon completing this chapter, you should be able to:

- Describe the public sector.

- Define fixed assets.

- Identify the types of fixed assets.

- Describe the reasons that the public sector manages fixed assets.

- Provide a general description of the fixed assets management principles.

- Briefly describe the fixed assets cost determinants.

- Identify the Federal grants management programs available.

Introduction

Fixed assets management activities are a meaningful part of the public sector functions. Good fixed assets management establishes and maintains a current inventory of personal property used within the organization. In so doing, responsibility and accountability for personal property is established to ensure effective and efficient usage of the property. Additionally, a good fixed assets management program will facilitate the physical inventory of fixed assets, advance the establishment of insurance conditions, and comply with federal, state, or local policy.

Fixed assets management is not the only name for this segment of the materials management area. It has had a number of titles through the years. Property management is a common title used in the public sector. Other names used are equipment management, and, to a lesser degree, inventory control, although that name is normally reserved for the management of expendable supplies for use within the organization. The National Institute of Governmental Purchasing, Inc. uses the title fixed assets management in its Inventory and Warehouse Management Seminar.[1] Fixed assets management appears to be in common usage with software manufacturers who develop inventory and tracking software for personal property. In this book the title fixed assets management is used throughout to describe the process of managing personal property. This title appears to more adequately describe this function in the public sector. However, property, equipment, and fixed assets are used interchangeably to describe fixed assets.

The fixed assets manager, individual responsible for fixed assets management, is continuously encountering a diversity of challenges involving technology, administration, personnel, and management functions. In order to direct the fixed asset management effort of their organization, the manager must understand the organization's operating policies and procedures. The complexity and value of personal property has dramatically increased in recent years, as a result, the new fixed assets manager is finding it more and more difficult to learn the skills of managing the fixed assets program. This effort necessitates more planning and expertise on the part of the manager. The fixed assets program must be dynamic rather than static, proactive rather than reactive, and accommodating to changes in organizational needs rather than unaccommodating.

Fixed assets managers play a key role in today's materials management structure, whether they are at the federal, state, or local level. In today's materials management environment, the fixed assets manager is confronted with recognizing the need for education and information in a rapidly changing environment and organization. The fixed assets manager must be a dynamic supervisor, an organizer, a self-starter, and a generalist who is willing to get out and take charge.

What Is The Public Sector

The Code of Federal Regulations, Title 41, Volume 2, Chapter 101, Section 101-43.001-26 defines public agency as: "any State; political subdivision thereof, including any unit of local government or economic development district; any department, agency, or instrumentality thereof, including instrumentalities created by compact or other agreement between States or political subdivisions; multijurisdictional substate districts established by or pursuant to State law; or any Indian tribe, band, group, pueblo, or community located on a State reservation."

In broad terms, the public sector encompasses all of the governmental agencies that provide the common goods and services that the taxpaying public needs. This segment includes federal, state, county, city, and municipalities that carry out the missions of government. The public sector can be viewed as all governmental agencies including higher education, hospitals, and the other non-profit organizations in federal, state, county, and city government. The distinction between private organizations and the public sector is that of the profit motive. Private organizations are in business to compete and return a profit for their stockholders. Whereas, the public sector is often classified as non-profit organizations and are chartered to provide services to their constituents. The public sector is itself

3

governed by the laws passed by the legislature or governing boards and commissions. Elected officials often are the top managers of public sector agencies and lend a challenging element to the equation. Public agencies often have the special attention of the elected officials, the public, and the press, which have a stake in assuring the accountability of government to the people.

Accountability is a key feature of the public sector and one of the principal arguments taken into account in this book. The public sector is answerable to the taxpayers such that it must aspire to policies that are compatible with public desires. The people are the pivotal element in a democracy and those in the public sector are accountable to all of the people in a democracy. There is, however, an underlying distrust of the public sector by the people. Therefore, most programs and policies in government contain numerous control programs and a high degree of accountability. Fixed assets management is no exception. The primary purpose for fixed assets management is to ensure accountability of the significant investment in assets entrusted to the public sector administrators.

What Are Fixed Assets

Fixed assets are many things to the many public sector entities and are, in all probability, as variously defined. It can be any item costing over a certain dollar amount, large or small, to an item that has a certain useful life. A public sector organization's assets represent a substantial financial investment. The costs of acquiring, maintaining, insuring, and replacing these assets have a considerable impact on the operations of the entity. Fixed assets are not always found in one place and, in fact, are more commonly thought of as movable assets, property, or equipment. As movable assets, they get transferred from place to place creating a management challenge. Assets also tends to be used up or expended over time and their value declines to the point where they are no longer thought of as assets and can be thought of as an albatross or burden on the organization. At the end of their useful life, most assets are apt to have some scrap or salvage value depending on the asset and, therefore, become an interesting challenge for the fixed assets manager.

To define fixed assets one must look at a number of definitions and combine the definitions to form one meaningful definition that will apply to the particular circumstances of the public sector. The Merriam-Webster Dictionary defines property as "something owned or possessed, a piece of real estate; the exclusive right to possess, enjoy, and dispose of a thing; something to which a person or business has a legal title." Personal property is defined as "property other than real property consisting of things temporary or movable." The dictionary further defines equipment as " the implements used in the operation or activity; all the fixed assets other than land and buildings of a business enterprise." [2]

The Concise Columbia Electronic Encyclopedia defines property as "in law, the right of ownership, i.e., the exclusive right to possess, enjoy, and dispose of an object of value; also, the object of value possessed, enjoyed, and disposed of by right of ownership. Modern Anglo-American property law provides for ownership of nearly all things of economic value; there are exceptions, such as the high seas or outer space, which are not subject to ownership. The law divides property into realty (real property) and personalty (personal property). Realty is chiefly land improvements built thereon; personalty is chiefly movable objects whose distribution the owner can determine by sale, will, or gift. Realty, in medieval times, was the basis of wealth and the keystone of the social structure; its ownership was controlled to protect society. The ownership of personalty, being of minor importance, was almost unfettered. With the rise of commerce and a large landless middle class, personalty became the dominant form of property, and the law of realty gradually became assimilated in most respects into that of personality."[3]

Figure 1-1: Examples of Public Sector Assets

Fixed assets, from the definitions above, can be thought of as something owned or possessed, something to which the public organization has legal title, is other than real property consisting of things temporary or movable, and all the property other than land and buildings of a public organization. Normally, the property managed is defined as personal property as opposed to real property. Therefore, real property and those items attached to the real property are usually not included in the definition of fixed assets. It is those assets that are movable or used temporarily that lend themselves to being managed. Examples of fixed assets include computers, furniture, printers, vehicles, boats, motors, analyzers, microscopes, medical equipment, education equipment, athletic equipment, and roadway equipment. Expendable supplies that are expended upon use, such as, pens, pencils, nuts, bolts, pipe, oil, gas, and valves are not fixed assets.

The definitions gleaned from the dictionary and encyclopedia are good, rough definitions that describe fixed assets in general terms. We must delve further into the subject to obtain a suitable definition that will serve the needs of public sector fixed asset management to its fullest.

The Federal Government's Office of Management and Budget (OMB) publishes the OMB Circular A-21 to establish principles for determining costs applicable to grants, contracts, and other agreements with educational institutions. The principles deal with the subject of cost determination and make no attempt to identify the circumstances or dictate the extent of agency and institutional participation in the financing of a particular project. The principles are designed to ensure that the Federal Government bear its fair share of total costs, determined in accordance with generally accepted accounting principles, except where restricted or prohibited by law. Agencies are not expected to place additional restrictions on individual items of cost. OMB Circular A-21 defines equipment as: "Equipment" means an article of nonexpendable, tangible personal property having a useful life of more than one year and an acquisition cost which equals or exceeds the lesser of the capitalization level established by the organization for financial statement purposes, or $5,000.[4]

Additionally, the Office of Management and Budget publishes OMB Circular A-110 that sets forth standards for obtaining consistency and uniformity among Federal agencies in the administration of grants and agreements with institutions of higher education, hospitals, and other non-profit organizations. OMB Circular A-110 defines equipment as: Equipment means tangible nonexpendable personal property including exempt property charged directly to the award having a useful life of more than one year and an acquisition cost of $5,000 or more per unit. However, consistent with recipient policy, lower limits may be established.[5]

Both of the above definitions introduced two additional terms to the dictionary and encyclopedia definitions. This is the first that "useful life" and "acquisition cost" have been mentioned. These two terms furnish more depth to our rudimental dictionary definition. Fixed assets, according to the OMB, must now have some minimum useful life and cost before they may b classified as truly being fixed assets. The Office of Management and Budget, to consider an item as fixed assets, calls for a useful life of one year. The OMB's conditions apply to institutions of higher education, hospitals, and other non-profit organizations. That would seem to include all organizations in the public sector. Therefore, if a public sector organization intends to obtain a grant or agreement with the Federal Government, its definition of fixed assets must include a useful life of at least one-year. Using the same reasoning, the fixed asset must have a minimum acquisition cost of $5,000 to be classified as fixed assets. The public organization may set lower capitalization limits; however, if applying for a grant, the minimum limit will be $5,000 or additional approval will be needed.

Armed with this further information, we can now define fixed assets for the public sector. Fixed asset means "personal property that is not permanently attached to real property, buildings or grounds; that is movable; has a useful life of at least one year and a minimum acquisition cost established by the organization." The minimum acquisition cost, as we know from above, must be $5,000 to be qualified by the Federal Government as a fixed asset; however, we will leave the establishment of a minimum acquisition cost open for the organization to determine. The organization may wish to establish a lower minimum acquisition cost for tracking and accountability purposes. The above definition provides the organization the flexibility to adequately identify and manage its fixed assets.

Types Of Fixed Assets

Fixed assets encompass a wide variety of assets, Figure 1-1. They may be standard off-the-shelf items, such as, forklifts, automobiles, computers, printing presses, and laboratory equipment. Other assets may be significantly modified or custom made for a particular purpose. Robots, specialized medical equipment are examples of such specialized assets. The list could grow much larger depending on the dollar limit established by the agency to be considered an asset. If the dollar limit is set low, below $500, for example, the list of assets will grow astronomically and the task of accounting for the assets will also increase. As the dollar limit is increased, the list of the types of fixed assets will decrease proportionally.

There are three major characteristics of fixed assets. These characteristics are:

They are acquired for use in operations and not for resale. Only assets used in normal business operations should be classified as fixed assets.

They are long-term in nature. Fixed assets yield services over a number of years.

They possess physical substance. Fixed assets are characterized by physical existence or substance and thus are differentiated from intangible assets, such as patents and goodwill.[6]

Why Manage Fixed Assets

As stated earlier, fixed assets represents a significant dollar investment for any public sector organization. In public utility companies, for example, net plant assets (plant assets less accumulated depreciation) often represent more than 75% of total assets. Recently, net plant assets were 79% of Consolidated Edison's total assets and 92% of Pennsylvania Power & Light Company's.[7] It is important that the fixed assets be accounted for as they are being used within the organization. According to the Code of Federal Regulations, Title 41, Volume 2, Chapter 101, Section 101-

43.001-18 management means the safeguarding of the government's interest in property in an efficient and economical manner consistent with the best business practices. Fixed asset management fits very well within this definition. A fixed asset management program is important for a number of reasons. Most evident is its importance in the control of losses due to pilferage, theft, and neglect. Losses are controllable and can be prevented or minimized. Reliable fixed asset management programs have an additional fundamental value in the maximization of the use of assets by facilitating sharing between and within departments and subdivisions. Scarce resources in the public sector are a reality and it's highly likely that only one of a particular asset may be affordable to the organization for use in a number of departments or subdivisions.

Another point of view that commands serious attention is the importance of an accurate fixed asset management program to meet the growing demands from federal and state-funding sources for improved control and accountability over fixed assets. It is important that the worth of the accountability over assets does not become the basis for the rejection of government grants, contracts, and appropriations. In addition, OMB Circular A-110 and other government regulations covering administration of agreements with federal government agencies require that public agencies avoid purchasing "unnecessary or duplicative items."[8] Federal agencies have the authority to disallow reimbursement for new assets when suitable assets are already available. A reliable and accurate fixed asset management program will ensure that such requests will not be rejected.

Public sector managers, administrators and employees have a duty and responsibility to provide protection for the assets under their control. This protection is for losses from natural disasters, theft, fire, and an abundance of other ills that can befall a public sector organization. Protection is provided in the way of insurance on the fixed assets to provide for replacement if damaged or destroyed. Accurate fixed asset records are necessary to prove the severity of the losses once they have occurred. The fixed asset management program ensures accurate documentation for such an eventuality.

A major purpose of a fixed asset management program is to establish and assign responsibility for the assets. This purpose aligns with the accountability philosophy previously discussed. From a functional perspective, accountability has been presented in the form of a ladder comprising five distinct levels. The levels move from more objectively measured aspects (legal compliance) to aspects requiring more subjective measures (policies pursued and rejected). The ladder is generally consistent with the analysis of the American Accounting Association's (AAA) Committee of Concepts of Accounting Applicable to the Public Sector.

Level 1: Policy accountability-selection of policies pursued and rejected (value)

Level 2: Program accountability-establishment and achievement of goals (outcomes and effectiveness)

Level 3: Performance accountability-efficient operation (efficiency and economy)

Level 4: Process accountability-using adequate processes, procedures, or measures in performing the actions called for (planning, allocating, and managing)

Level 5: Probity and legality accountability-spending funds in accordance with the approved budget or being in compliance with laws and regulations (compliance)[9]

The public sector has not been saddled with the task of computing depreciation on its assets. Generally accepted accounting practices have not compelled that non-profit governmental organizations compute and track depreciation. However, this rule has recently changed and all not-for-profit organizations will be required to recognize the cost of using up long-lived tangible assets-depreciation-in general-purpose external financial statements. With the obligation for the public sector to account for depreciation, the burden of providing positive inventory and tracking of fixed assets will fall on the fixed asset management function.

Fixed Asset Management Organization

Is there a standard organizational placement for the fixed asset management function in the public sector? This question could be researched for years without adequately answering the question because of the wide diversity in public sector organizations. To understand the enormity of the task one must gain insight to the organizing function. Increasing specialization of activities, projects, and skills demand that managers look to elements within their control for gaining coordination by designing, mapping out, and deliberately planning the duties and relationships of people in the organization. In summary, the organizing function seeks:

To establish efficient and logical patterns of interrelationships among members of the organization.

To secure advantages of specialization whereby the optimum utilization of talents can be realized.

To coordinate activities of the component parts in order to facilitate the realization of the goals of the organization. [10]

In some organizations, the fixed assets manager is in the controller's office and is responsible for the inventory and tracking of assets, as well as, the fixed assets accounting functions. There are other organizations where the function reports directly to a chief executive officer such as a vice president. Still other public agencies have the fixed asset management function reporting to the chief procurement officer; Figure 1-2 shows a typical organization structure of

12

that nature. This type of organizational placement ranks fixed asset management on the same level and status as the other functions within the procurement department. The director of procurement reports to a vice president who has equal status as the other vice presidents providing the power to operate within the organization with a high level of status and power. This type of organization seems to fulfill the organizing functional requirements listed above.

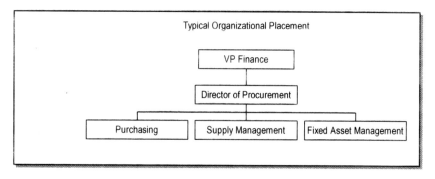

Figure 1-2: Fixed Asset Management Organizational Placement

Regardless of the organizational placement of the fixed asset management function, there should be an organization chart that accurately shows the lines of authority, responsibility, and accountability for the function. The primary purposes to chart the organization structure are to show the hierarchical way functions and individuals have been grouped together, including the authority and responsibility lines that connect them. Organizational charts, to be useful, must show "what is" as opposed to "what should be." There are six principles proposed by classical writers of organization design. Although these principles are no longer interpreted to be universally applicable for all organizations, they continue to offer a foundation upon which managers can build a workable structure.[11]

One of the traditional principles generally referred to as *unity of command*, states that no member of an organization should report to more than one supervisor on any single function. The application of this principle is easy in a pure line organization, in which each superior has general authority; however, it becomes a complex problem in actual cases in which some form of staff and/or functional organization is used. In practice, instructions may be received from several sources without the loss of productivity. The central problem is to avoid conflict in orders from different people relating to the same subject. You should recognize immediately that many people who are not recognized in the formal hierarchy of authority might influence the actions of a subordinate. The unity-of-command principle simply means that subordinates need to know from whom they receive the authority to make decisions and take action.

The *exception principle* states that lower-level managers should handle recurring decisions in a routine manner, whereas problems involving unusual matters should be referred to higher levels. This principle emphasizes that executives at the top levels of an organization have limited time and capacity and should refrain from becoming bogged down in routine details that can be handled as well by subordinates.

A third principle involves the *span of control* of a manger: there is a limit to the number of subordinates that one superior should supervise. The determination of the optimum number depends on many factors in a given organization and should always be tied directly to the question of the number of levels in the hierarchy. If it appears that a small span of control for each manager is desirable, then the number of necessary levels will be larger than would be the case with a larger span of control. The organization with more levels is considered "tall," whereas the organization with a larger span of control is "flat." A tall structure with small spans of control assumes that coordination can be attained only by direct supervision. A flat structure with large spans of control assumes that mutual adjustment among subordinates can handle much of the coordination of members.

A fourth principle, the **scalar principle,** states that authority and responsibility should flow in a clear, unbroken line, or chain of command, from the highest to the lowest manager. The principle simply states that an organization is a hierarchy. The importance and usefulness of the principle is evident whenever the line is severed. The splintering of one organization into two or more results from a permanent breach of this principle. Temporary breaches, however, are not uncommon, although they are frequently subtle and unrecognized. The tendency of an aggressive executive to fight the control of superiors can create an environment for forming an "empire" that is uncoordinated with the larger organization.

The manner in which activities should be divided and formed into specialized groups is referred to as **departmentation.** The purpose of departmentation is to specialize activities, simplify the tasks of managers, and retain control. Several types of departmentation are possible: geographical, by customer, by process or equipment, by product, or by professional skills. Often, different types are used at different levels of the organization structure.

In the organizational sense, **decentralization** is the process of diversifying and delegating authority to lower-level managers. Centralization and decentralization are matters of degree; they should be treated as two ends of a continuum. Two important considerations determine the degree of decentralization desirable in a given situation. First, the amount of skills and competence possessed by subordinate managers influences the success of any program of decentralization; managers must be developed who can adequately handle the authority delegated to them. Second, the distribution of the necessary information to points of decision is critical to any delegation process; an executive with insufficient information available for making a decision will have little chance to make a good one.

Fixed Asset Management Principles

A fixed asset management program is effective and efficient if it facilitates the attainment of the goals and objective of the organization. The matter of effectiveness and efficiency are variously open to interpretation and will depend on the individuals and agencies involved. There are certain fixed asset management principles that can be used as a guide for public sector agencies to use in managing their asset investment. These principles assist in meeting the goals and objectives of the organization, in effective and efficient operation of the fixed asset program, in making sound decisions, in reducing costs, and in providing incentives for management improvements. The fixed asset management principles are:

Maximize the taxpayer's dollars: Taxpayers dollars are always to be maximized in the public sector. Money is a scarce resource is a well-used and true axiom in the public sector. Fixed asset managers must be aware of the scarceness of funds and strive to maximize the use of all assets.

Make surplus assets the first source of supply: Fixed asset managers must promote the usage of surplus assets. Policies and procedures must be established for the purchasing department and other agency departments requiring that surplus assets be reviewed and used prior to purchasing new assets.

Maximize the reuse of fixed assets: A sound policy to reuse assets is needed. Performance measurements should be established and performance reports developed measuring the number of assets reused within the agency. Departments reusing assets should be given credit for their performance thus assuring future performance.

Manage the fixed asset program effectively and efficiently: Effectively and efficiently are two very overused words in public agencies. However, they definitely have desired connotations. If one is effective, they are thought of as producing a decided, decisive, or desired effect and if one is efficient, they can be though of as being productive without waste. It is easy to understand why managers tend to use the two words collectively and it is just as easy to see why managers would apply them to fixed asset management.

Trained fixed asset managers provide superior services: The fixed asset manager is continuously encountering a diversity of challenges involving technology, administration, personnel, and management functions. In order to direct the fixed asset management effort of his or her organization, the manager must be adequately trained to meet these challenges. The complexity and value of the fixed asset management job has dramatically increased in recent years, as a result, the fixed asset manager is finding it more and more difficult to learn the skills of managing the fixed asset program.

Fixed Asset Cost Determination

Fixed asset costs are determined in accordance with the cost principle of accounting. Costs consist of all expenditures necessary to acquire the asset and make it ready for its intended use. For example, the purchase costs, freight costs, paid by the purchaser, and installation costs are all considered part of the cost of the asset.

Cost is measured by the cash paid in a cash transaction or by the cash equivalent price paid when noncash assets are used in payment. The cash equivalent is equal to the fair market value of the asset given up or the fair market value of the asset received whichever is more clearly determinable. Once cost is established, it becomes the basis of accounting for the asset over its useful life. Current market or replacement values are not used.

The cost consists of the cash price, sales taxes, freight charges, and insurance during transit paid by the purchaser. It also includes expenditures used in assembling, installing and testing the unit. However, motor vehicle licenses and accident insurance on agency trucks and cars are not included because they represent annual recurring expenditures and do not benefit future periods.[12]

Assume that a university print shop purchases a new printing press at a cost of $78,450. Other expenses include sales taxes of $4,707, installation and testing of $7,845, training of $5,500 and startup supplies of $2,456. The acquisition cost would consist of the cash price, sales taxes, installation, and testing cost as indicated below.

The costs of training and startup supplies are not included in the acquisition cost. These costs are not recurring cost to future periods and are, therefore, eliminated from the acquisition cost. The situation may be complicated when using a trade-in to offset the acquisition cost.

Printing Press	
Printing Press	$78,450
Sales taxes	4,707
Installation and testing	7,845
Acquisition cost	$91,002

Using the same printing press as an example, assume that an old printing press is traded-in on the new printing press and the seller allows $10,100 dollars toward the purchase of the new press. The acquisition cost would be computed as follows:

Printing Press	
Printing Press	$78,450
Less Trade-in	<10,100>
Sub total	68,350
Sales taxes	4,101
Installation and testing	7,845
Acquisition cost	$90,396

The acquisition cost is computed on the cash price before trade-in. The difference in acquisition cost is due to the sales taxes being computed on the after trade-in price.

During the useful life of an asset a jurisdiction may incur costs for ordinary repairs, additions, and improvements. Ordinary repairs are expenditures to maintain the operating efficiency and expected productive life of the asset. They usually are of small amounts that occur frequently throughout service life. Motor tune-ups and oil changes, painting of equipment, and the replacement of worn-out gears on machinery are examples. These expenditures do not change the useful life of the asset and, therefore, do not change the value of the asset.

Additions and improvements are costs incurred to increase the operating efficiency, productive capacity, or expected useful life of the asset. These expenditures are usually material in amount and occur infrequently during the life of the asset. Expenditures for additions and improvements increase the investment in the asset.[13]

An addition generally results in a larger physical unit and increased productive capacity. Improvement results in the replacement of a subunit with a new unit. For example, a computer with a 1-MB hard drive may be improved by replacing the hard drive with a 3-MB hard drive. Expenditures for additions and improvements increase the overall value of the asset. Therefore, the value of such assets must be increased to account for the addition or improvement.

Grants

A grant is used when the principal purpose of a transaction is to accomplish a public purpose of support or stimulation authorized by Federal statute. Public sector agencies depend heavily on Federal grants of fixed assets and the Federal Government has programs available to assist public sector agencies. The Office of Management and Budget is the federal agency tasked with managing the grant programs. Specifically, the Office of Management and Budget, working cooperatively with Federal agencies and non-Federal parties, establishes government wide grants management policies and guidelines through circulars and common rules. There are five Office of Management and Budget circulars of interest to the public sector in obtaining and managing Federal grants.

OMB Circular A-21, Principles for Determining Costs Applicable to Grants, Contracts and Other Agreements With Educational Institutions:[14] These principles provide principles for determining the costs applicable to research and development, training, and other sponsored work performed by colleges and universities under grants, contracts, and other agreements with the Federal Government. These agreements are referred to as sponsored agreements. These principles are used in determining the allowable costs of work performed by colleges and universities under sponsored agreements. The principles are also used in determining the costs of work performed by such institutions under subgrants, cost-reimbursement subcontracts, and other awards made under sponsored agreements. They also can be used as a guide in the pricing of fixed-price contracts and subcontracts where costs are used in determining the appropriate price.

OMB Circular A-87, Cost Principles for State, Local and Indian Tribal Governments:[15] This Circular establishes principles and standards to provide a uniform approach for determining costs and to promote effective program delivery, efficiency, and better relationships between governmental units and the Federal Government. The principles are for determining allowable costs only. They are not intended to identify the circumstances or to dictate the extent of Federal and governmental unit participation in the financing of a particular Federal award. Provision for profit or other increment above cost is outside the scope of this Circular.

OMB Circular A-102, Grants and Cooperative Agreements with State and Local Governments:[16] This Circular establishes consistency and uniformity among Federal agencies in the management of grants and cooperative agreements with State, local, and federally-recognized Indian tribal governments. On March 12, 1987, the President directed all affected agencies to issue a grants management common rule to adopt government-wide terms and conditions for grants to State and local governments, and they did so. In 1988, OMB revised the Circular to provide guidance to Federal agencies on other matters not covered in the common rule. Consistent with their legal obligations, all Federal agencies administering programs that involve grants and cooperative agreements with State, local and Indian tribal governments (grantees) shall follow the policies in this Circular.

OMB Circular A-110, Uniform Administrative Requirements for Grants and Agreements with Institutions of Higher Education, Hospitals, and Other Non-Profit Organizations.[17] This Circular establishes uniform administrative requirements for Federal grants and agreements awarded to institutions of higher education, hospitals, and other non-profit organizations. OMB Circular 110 states that grant recipients shall have effective control over and accountability for all funds, property, and other assets received under grant. Additionally, recipients are required to adequately safeguard all such assets and assure they are used solely for authorized purposes. The circular contains some important definitions and procedures for the fixed assets manager. Definitions are included for Acquisition Cost, Equipment, Excess Property, Exempt Property, Intangible Property, Personal Property, Property, And Supplies. Procedures included provide the manner that public sector organizations will use in dealing with the granting agencies to ensure fairness to all. Furthermore, the circular contains procedures regarding titling considerations; proper use of equipment; equipment records required; control systems to adequate safeguards to prevent loss, damage, or theft; and disposition instructions.

OMB Circular A-122, Cost Principles for Non-Profit Organizations:[18] This Circular establishes principles for determining costs of grants, contracts, and other agreements with nonprofit organizations. It does not apply to colleges and universities that are covered by Circular A-21; State, local, and federally recognized Indian tribal governments which are covered by Circular 74-4; or hospitals. The principles are designed to provide that the Federal Government bear its fair share of costs except where restricted or prohibited by law. The principles do not attempt to prescribe the extent of cost sharing or matching on grants, contracts, or other agreements.

OMB Circular A-133, Audits of States, Local Governments, and Non-Profit Organizations:[19] This Circular is applied by all Federal agencies. It sets forth standards for obtaining consistency and uniformity among Federal agencies for the audit of non-Federal entities expending Federal awards. Federal agencies apply the provisions of this Circular to non-Federal entities, whether they are recipients expending Federal awards received directly from Federal awarding agencies, or are subrecipients expending Federal awards received from a pass-through entity (a recipient or another subrecipient).

Summary

This chapter completes the introduction to fixed asset management. In this chapter the public sector was defined as well as the development of a definition of fixed assets in the public sector. The public sector was defined as encompassing all of the governmental agencies that provide the common goods and services that the taxpaying public demands. Fixed assets was defined as personal property that is not permanently attached to real property, buildings or grounds, that is movable, has a useful life of at least one year and a minimum acquisition cost established by the organization.

The importance of managing the public sector assets was explored. The concern of the taxpayers for adequate control and accountability for these expensive and, in some cases, critical assets was discussed. Public sector managers and administrators are said to have a duty and responsibility to provide protection for the assets under their control. With this in mind, a primary purpose for a fixed asset management program is to establish and assign responsibility for the assets.

The organizational placement of the fixed asset management function was researched. The fixed asset function calls for assignment at an organization level that can command cooperation from all agency departments. Regardless of the organizational placement of the fixed asset management function, there should be an organization chart that accurately shows the lines of authority, responsibility, and accountability for the function. The primary purposes to chart the organization structure are to show the hierarchical way functions and individuals have been grouped together, including the authority and responsibility lines that connect them.

A fixed asset management program is effective and efficient if it facilitates the attainment of the goals and objective of the organization. The matter of effectiveness and efficiency are variously open to interpretation and will depend on the individuals and agencies involved. There are five fixed asset management principles that can be used as a guide for public sector agencies to use in managing their fixed asset investment.

Maximize the taxpayer's dollars.

Make surplus assets the first choice of supply.

Maximize the reuse of fixed assets.

Manage the fixed asset program efficiently and effectively.

Trained fixed asset managers provide superior service.

Fixed asset costs are determined in accordance with the cost principle of accounting. Costs consist of all expenditures necessary to acquire the asset and make it ready for its intended use. For example, the purchase price, freight costs, paid by the purchaser, and installation costs are all considered part of the cost of the asset.

A grant is used when the principal purpose of a transaction is to accomplish a public purpose of support or stimulation authorized by Federal statute. Public sector agencies depend heavily on Federal grants of fixed assets and the Federal Government has programs available to assist public sector agencies. The Office of Management and Budget is the federal agency tasked with managing the grant programs.

Questions

1. Briefly describe the makeup of the public sector.

2. Define personal property

3. Identify the various types of fixed assets found in public sector agencies.

4. Briefly explain why the public sector manages fixed assets.

5. Where is the fixed asset management function normally assigned in the public sector and why.

6. List the fixed asset management principles.

7. What factors are included in the cost of accountable assets?

8. List the five Office of Management and Budget circulars pertaining to grants management.

Notes

---

[1] *Inventory and Warehouse Management*, (National Institute of Governmental Purchasing, Inc., 1991).

[2] WWWebster Dictionary, (http://www.m-w.com/cgi-bin/dictionary).

[3] Encyclopedia.com – Results for property, (http://www.encyclopedia.com/articles/10553.html).

[4] OMB Circular A-21 (revised 10/27/98), *Cost Principles for Educational Institutions*, (Office of Management and Budget, Washington, DC, 1998).

[5] OMB Circular A-110 (Revised 11/19/93, As Further Amended 8/29/97), *Uniform Administrative Requirements for Grants and Agreements With Institutions of Higher Education, Hospitals, and Other Non-Profit Organizations*, (Office of Management and Budget, Washington, DC, 1993).

[6] Donald E. Kieso and Jerry J. Weygandt, *Intermediate Accounting*, (John Wiley & Sons, Inc., New York, 1995), 481.

[7] Jerry J. Weygandt, Donald E. Kieso and Walter G. Kell, *Accounting Principles*, (John Wiley & Sons, Inc., New York, 1993) 398.

[8] OMB Circular A-110 (Revised 11/19/93, As Further Amended 8/29/97), *Uniform Administrative Requirements for Grants and Agreements With Institutions of Higher Education, Hospitals, and Other Non-Profit Organizations*, (Office of Management and Budget, Washington, DC, 1993).

[9] *Accountability*, (http://www.rutgers.edu/Acconting/raw/gasb/seagov/accounta.htm).

[10] Joseph L. Massie and John Douglas, *Managing, a contemporary introduction*, (Prentice-Hall, Inc., Englewood Cliffs, NJ 1973), 267.

[11] Massie and Douglas, *Managing, a contemporary introduction*, 272.

[12] Jerry J. Weygandt, Donald E. Kieso and Walter G. Kell, *Accounting Principles*, (John Wiley & Sons, Inc., New York, 1993) 399-400.

[13] Weygandt, Kieso and Kell, *Accounting Principles*, 412.

[14] OMB Circular A-21 (revised 10/27/98), *Cost Principles for Educational Institutions*, (Office of Management and Budget, Washington, DC, 1998).

[15] OMB Circular A-87, *Cost Principles for State, Local and Indian Tribal Governments*, (Office of Management and Budget, Washington, DC, 1995).

[16] OMB Circular A-102, *Grants and Cooperative Agreements with State and Local Governments*, (Office of Management and Budget, Washington, DC, 1994).

[17] OMB Circular A-110 (Revised 11/19/93, As Further Amended 8/29/97), *Uniform Administrative Requirements for Grants and Agreements With Institutions of Higher Education, Hospitals, and Other Non-Profit Organizations*, (Office of Management and Budget, Washington, DC, 1993).

[18] OMB Circular A-122, *Cost Principles for Non-Profit Organizations*, (Office of Management and Budget, Washington, DC, 1998).

[19] OMB Circular A-133, *Audits of States, Local Governments, and Non-Profit Organizations*, (Office of Management and Budget, Washington, DC, 1997).

Chapter 2 Control And Accountability

Purpose

This chapter analyzes the control and accountability interfaces that the fixed asset management department encounters internally with other departments.

Objectives

Upon completing this chapter, you should be able to:

- Explain the enabling legislation for the fixed asset management department.
- Name the ten control functions.
- Briefly describe accountability as it pertains to fixed asset management.
- Differentiate the levels of assignment of responsibility for fixed assets.
- Explain how the capitalization policy affects fixed asset management.
- Describe the identification and tagging process.

Introduction

The purpose of fixed asset management is to secure control and accountability over assets. The process includes assigning responsibility for assets by designating individuals to be responsible for assets during their useful life, tagging assets in a positive manner to identify the asset, and maintaining records on all assets. Fixed asset management must have the proper authority based on a resolution, charter, statute or legislation to operate within the organization. It is important that the authority be written such that fixed asset management will be able to control and account for the organization's assets.

Control is used to detect possible or actual departure from policies or procedures and in the end to allow for effective corrective action. Devices used in the control function are the policies and procedures for safeguarding the agency's assets, the fixed assets records and other information management tools. Additionally, control is one of the major functions of management dealing with making control devices and practices fit in with plans and the organizational structure. Effective controls entail consistency with the organizational goals and objectives, establishment of operational responsibility, ability to comprehend the needs for policies and procedures and needs of the individuals assigned fixed assets responsibilities.

Accountability is a key feature of the public sector. The public sector is answerable to the taxpayers such that it must aspire to policies that are compatible with public desires. There is an underlying distrust of the public sector by the people. Therefore, most programs and policies in government contain numerous control programs and a high degree of accountability. Fixed assets management is no exception. A primary purpose of fixed assets management is to ensure accountability of the significant investment in fixed assets entrusted to the public sector administrators. As stated earlier, fixed assets represents a significant dollar investment for any public sector organization. It is important that the assets be accounted for as they are being used within the organization. Another purpose of a fixed assets management program is to establish and assign responsibility for the assets. This purpose aligns with the accountability philosophy previously discussed.

Authority

To be effective the fixed assets management program must be based on a resolution, charter, specific statutes, or legislation. The authorizing legislation may be very specific as to the fixed assets management methods and restrictive as to the extent of the authority that may be delegated. However, the overall purpose should not be to restrict operations, but to gather and maintain information needed for the preparation of financial statements and to afford control and accountability over fixed assets while preventing loss and abuse. Legislation should represent the minimum fixed assets management requisites to be met by the public sector agencies. The agency may maintain its fixed assets management system in greater detail than that called for by legislation but not below those established minimums.

In addition to appropriate legislation supporting the fixed assets management function, there should, also, be written policies and procedures to govern the day-to-day operations. Policies are considered broad guidelines to activities and to the development of operating procedures. Top management establishes policies that govern the fixed assets management function, such as, those concerning how transfers will be handled. Established policies must be consistent with the fixed assets management function's goals and objectives and with agency policies governing the fixed assets management function.

The fixed assets manager usually establishes the operating procedures. Policies, as we have seen, guide the fixed assets manager in making decisions and taking actions that lead toward organizational goals and objective. Procedures are the detailed steps to be taken in order to accomplish the job. Procedures answer the "how to" questions. Such questions as, how to identify assets, how to effect the transfer of assets and how to assign responsibility for assets are answered in the fixed assets management operating procedures.

The following are general subjects that should be included in the procedures manual:

Goals and Objectives: State the goals and objectives of the fixed assets management program.

Purpose: State the purpose of the fixed assets management program, such as, better utilization of assets, establish insurance requirements, etc.

General Definitions: Define fixed assets, capitalization, and other key terms.

Responsibility: Establish the responsibility for fixed assets from the lowest echelon to the highest.

Personal Use Of Fixed Assets: Indicate the agency policy on personal use of assets.

Control and Identification: State the methods to ensure positive control and identification over assets.

Donated Assets: Indicate how donated assets will be accepted and the establishment of fair market value for those assets.

Transfers: Describe how asset transfers between departments will be conducted.

Excess Property: Explain the procedures to follow in identifying, re-issuing and arranging for pickup and delivery of excess property.

Trade-in of Fixed Assets: Describe how to use asset for trade-in credit.

Lost, Missing, or Stolen Assets: State the procedures for investigating lost, missing, or stolen assets and the authority to remove the assets from inventory.

Annual Inventory Verification: Describe the procedures to be followed to perform annual inventory verifications.

Acquisition of State/Federal Surplus Property: State how the agency will acquire state or federal surplus property and how to establish the fair market value of such assets.

Surplus Property: This section should state the procedures for disposal of surplus property.

Control

Controlling is used to illustrate management's attempts to ensure that its policies, procedures and outcomes are in line with its service and financial goals and objectives. Harold Koonz and Cyril O'Donnell indicate that, "It is sometimes not realized that the control system used by managers, like any other control system, must be designed for the task it is intended to perform. While the principles of control are universal, the actual system compels special design. In this tailoring of control systems or techniques, there are certain requirements that the manager should keep in mind." Furthermore, they go on to describe the ten requirements of adequate control. [1]

Controls must reflect the nature and needs of the activity. All control systems should reflect the job they are to perform. A system useful for the county manager will almost certainly be different in scope and nature of a recreation department foreman. Controls of the accounting department will differ from those of the purchasing department and these from the controls of the engineering department. This is merely a reflection of plans: the more controls are designed to deal with and reflect the specific nature and structure of plans, the more effective they will serve the interests of the agency and its managers. Certain techniques, such as written procedures and policies, performance measurements and tagging of assets have general application in many situations. However, it should never be assumed that any of these widely used techniques are applicable in a given situation. The fixed assets manager must be aware of the strategic factors in his control procedures and operations requiring control and use the technique suited to them.

Controls should report deviations promptly. The ideal control system detects projected deviations before they actually occur. In any case the information must reach the manager in a timely manner so that he or she can head off failures. If failures are not reported expeditiously, the result will be a weak fixed assets accounting program. Accounting, having for its original and basic purpose the recording of transactions, naturally looks backwards. Moreover, in the attempt to make accounting data comprehensive and accurate, it often reaches the manager after the event. It does the manager little good to find in October that an asset was lost in July. Management information systems are speeding the process; however, the human element is still relied upon, as the responsible person has to recognize the asset is missing from its normal location. Therefore, prompt reporting is necessary to the successful fixed assets program.

Controls should be forward looking. Although ideal control is instantaneous, as in certain electronic controls, the facts of managerial life include a time lag between the deviation and corrected action. Perhaps the first principle of control is to detect potential or actual deviation from plans early enough to permit effective corrective action. The fixed assets manager, in striving to apply this principle, should be proactive and attempt to forecast possible failures prior to occurrence. Procedures should be developed to detect failures and report failures in a timely manner as they occur.

Controls should point up exceptions at critical points. The time-honored exception principle, that the manager should only watch for and deal with exceptions, is not enough for effective control. Some deviations from established procedures have little meaning and others have a great deal. Small deviations in certain areas have greater significance than larger deviations in other areas. The fixed assets manager, for example, might be concerned if assets are being loss at a greater rate in one department than another regardless of the number of assets owned. A department owning a large number of assets should not have a greater loss rate than a department with few assets.

Controls should be objective. Management necessarily has many subjective elements in it, but whether a department is doing a good job managing its assets should ideally not be a matter of subjective determination. Where controls are subjective, a manager's personality may influence judgements of performance inaccurately; but people have difficulty in explaining away objective control of their performance, particularly if the standards and measurements are kept up-to-date through periodic review. Objective control should be definite and determinable in a clear and positive way. Effective control calls for objective, accurate and suitable standards.

Controls should be flexible. Controls must remain workable in the face of changed plans, unforeseen circumstances, or outright failures. As Goetz[2] has remarked: "A complex program of managerial plans may fail in some particulars. The control system should report such failures, and should contain sufficient elements of flexibility to maintain managerial control of operations despite such failures." In other words, according to the principle of flexibility, if controls are to remain effective, despite failure or unforeseen changes of plans, flexibility is required in their design.

Controls should reflect the organizational pattern. Organizational structure, being the principal vehicle for coordinating the work of people, is also a major means for maintaining control; and the manager is the focal point of control, just as he or she is the focal point for the assignment of tasks and the delegation of authority. This need is summarized in the principle of organizational suitability: the more controls are designed to reflect the place in the organization structure where responsibility for action lies, the more they will facilitate correction of deviations from plans.

Controls should be economical. Controls must be worth their cost. Although this requirement is simple, its practice is often complex, for a manager may find it difficult to know what a particular control system is worth, or to know what it costs. Economy is relative, since the benefits vary with the importance of the activity, the size of the operation, the expense that might be incurred in the absence of control, and the contribution the system can make.

Controls should be understandable. Some control systems, especially those based upon mathematical formulas, complex break-even charts, detailed analyses, and computer printouts, are not understandable to the managers who must use them. Sometimes the manager could understand them if he or she would take the time to learn to do so; but whether his or her lack of understanding results from complex techniques or impatience in learning them, the effect is the same: the control system will not function well.

Controls should lead to corrective action. A control system that detects deviations from plans will be little more than an interesting exercise if it does not show the way to corrective action. An adequate system will disclose where failures are occurring, who is responsible for them, and what should be done about them. It cannot be forgotten, as the principle of action emphasizes, that control is justified only if indicated or experienced deviations from plans are corrected through appropriate planning, organizing, staffing, and directing.

In fixed assets management a good control system is necessary to ensure that assets are properly accounted for, maintained in usable condition, prescribe uniform standards, and discourage pilferage. These controls should take into account the organizational structure and use the structure to assign the control responsibility for assets assigned to the organization. Controls must be placed on those assets requiring control and ignored on those that do not justify the cost of tracking. It is often more expensive to track an asset than it is to replace the asset. At one time electronic calculators were an item of great concern and were tracked as an asset. Today those same assets can be purchased for less than $50 making them a non-candidate for tracking. When controls are developed they must look ahead to the future. Controls that must be constantly changed tend to lose their credibility. Therefore, develop controls that have a long-range application. In the end develop controls that have the flexibility to allow the system to operate in a relative simple manner. Those control systems requiring a large number of forms, signatures and special routing should be avoided at all costs. Above all put Koonz and O'Donnell's ten requirements of adequate control in practical use and rely upon them to bestow adequate controls for the fixed assets management program.

Accountability

The term accountability is used to indicate a duty of a subordinate to carry out his or her duties. In military circles it is also used to dictate that an officer keeps accurate records and safeguard public fixed assets that is entrusted to them. Accountability involves the process by which a subordinate reports to a superior on the use of resources. Those resources may be fixed assets duly entrusted to a responsible person. Accountability, as stated earlier, forces the responsible person to keep accurate records. Fixed assets management is beset with records and the very nature of fixed assets management demands that all records, from cradle to grave, be accurately kept. Once a person is assigned the responsibility for fixed assets he or she must safeguard those assets against loss and practice loss prevention at all times. Fixed assets must be appropriately identified and marked in such a way as to ensure that loss can be detected. Assets must be stored where missing assets may be easily detected.

Accountability, a key feature of the public sector, places public sector managers answerable to the taxpayers such that they must aspire to accountability policies that are compatible with public desires. The people are the pivotal element in a democracy and those in the public sector are accountable to all of the people in a democracy. There is an underlying distrust of the public sector by the people. Therefore, most programs and policies in government contain a high degree of accountability. The people, as such, authorize the huge expenditure of public funds for fixed assets used in the public sector. The fixed assets management function, therefore, must ensure accountability of this significant investment. Public sector administrators are charged with this accountability function as a part of their employment agreement.

The Governmental Accounting Standards Board (GASB) Concepts Statement 1 describes accountability as a broad concept that forms the cornerstone of all financial reporting for state and local governmental entities. Although Concepts Statement 1 recognizes that financial reporting should supply information to assist users both in assessing accountability and in making economic, social, and political decisions, it states that accountability is the paramount objective from which all other objectives must flow. Accountability is a relationship between those who control or manage an entity and those who possess formal power over them. It forces the accountable party to give an explanation or a satisfactory reason for his or her activities and the results of efforts to achieve the specified tasks or objectives. Consistent with this notion, Concepts Statement 1 states that "accountability requires governments to answer to the citizenry—to justify the raising of public resources and the purposes for which they are used. Governmental accountability is based on the belief that the citizenry has a 'right to know,' a right to receive openly declared facts that may lead to public debate by the citizens and their elected representatives."

Governmental accounting is similar to private-sector accountability in that it includes an obligation to render an account or explain one's actions to someone else who has the authority or power to assess performance and to make a judgement and take action. The process includes (a) the necessity to render the elements of the account, (b) the analysis of that information and the making of a judgement by those to whom one is accountable, and (c) the exercise of power in the form of allocating praise or censure.[3]

There is a growing demand from federal and state-funding sources for improved accountability over fixed assets. The lack of an accurate accountability program over assets should not become the basis for the rejection of government grants, contracts, and appropriations. These programs are a valuable source of funds to public sector entities. A reliable and accurate fixed assets management program will ensure that such requests will not be rejected. Accountability assists in the assignment of responsibility for the fixed assets.

Centralized Versus Decentralized

An important issue in public sector organizations is whether the fixed assets management function should be centralized or decentralized. Centralized fixed assets management means that one special department handles fixed assets management. Decentralized fixed assets management means that individual agencies or departments handle their own fixed assets management functions.

There are several favorable attributes of centralized fixed assets management. Information management systems and computers are revolutionizing the traditional ways of accounting for fixed assets. Fixed assets managers control some of the public sector's most expensive and sensitive assets. Information systems, as well as fixed assets management, rely upon accurate data input to be useful. The centralized input of the fixed assets data is likely to be much more accurate if only one department is designated the responsibility for the input. The one department concept leads to better-trained individuals who input the data. An additional reason for centralized fixed assets management is to make available better service and closer attention to customer needs. Centralized fixed assets management often enables agencies to assign fixed assets specialists, who tend to be more efficient because they are able to concentrate their efforts on one function rather than spreading themselves across the departments.

Decentralized fixed assets management has the advantage of being better able to respond to departmental needs. Decentralized fixed assets management can usually offer quicker response to the physical inventory of fixed assets. Where departments are widely scattered, decentralized fixed assets management can perform the inventory in less time than the centralized function.

What is more prevalent is the combination of both centralization and decentralization by permitting departments to perform certain functions such as physical inventory while centralizing the overall responsibility.

Assigning Responsibility

Public sector personnel at all levels are responsible for the custody, maintenance and reasonable security for all fixed assets purchased for, or assigned to, their respective department or activity. Ownership of such fixed assets, however, rests with the federal, state, or local entity. This is true even if the assets are purchased with individual departmental funds or from special equipment appropriations or are acquired by gift, grant or contract. Table 2-1 lists the responsibility assignments for agency personnel.

All employees are responsible for the custody, maintenance and reasonable security of all fixed assets purchased for, or assigned to, their respective agency. They are also responsible for the proper care and security of any fixed assets that they may use or observe. Department heads are responsible for the custody, maintenance and reasonable security of all fixed assets purchased for, or assigned to, their respective department. The department head is the individual responsible for the overall operation of the respective department and the responsibility for the fixed assets assigned to the department is inherent to his or her duties.

All assets of an inventoriable nature must have a person responsible (custodian) for the use and upkeep of those assigned assets. The custodian is assigned by the department head and must be carefully selected on the basis of integrity, position, and trustworthiness. When assigned, the custodian is obligated to sign some form of acknowledgement indicating receipt and acceptance of the responsibility for the asset(s). Signature will, therefore, establish custodial responsibility. Custodians become responsible for the assets until duly relieved of their responsibility. They should secure written receipts relieving them of this responsibility when assets are removed from their area of responsibility.

The fixed assets management function is responsible for seeing that assets are inventoried, accounted for, and ultimately disposed of according to agency policies and procedures. Fixed assets management is responsible for maintaining a listing of all fixed assets assigned to the public sector agency, affixing identification tags to new acquisitions, reporting insurable values, and managing the annual inventory control program. Additionally, fixed assets management is responsible for giving guidance, assistance and information to upper management relative to the fixed assets program.

Assets donated to the agency, capital leased, self-constructed, or acquired other than by purchase should be accounted for in the same manner as purchased assets. Responsibility for such assets must be assigned and accounted for by signature establishing such responsibility in the same manner as purchased fixed assets. A responsible individual, other than the department head, should approve fixed assets received as a gift by the agency before acceptance. Such fixed assets should be accepted to fulfill a defined need and funding must be available to support such fixed assets. Otherwise, the assets will become an unnecessary burden on the agency.

There are occasions where the use of an asset may be needed on a temporary or semi-permanent basis by another agency, within or outside the organization. Policies and procedures must be in place to establish responsibility for assets during these temporary assignments. An agreement, defining responsibilities during the temporary custody period, should be in place. The agreement should indicate which agency will be responsible for the condition of the asset, upkeep, and insurance.

Public sector assets are for use primarily at the designated work place, however, certain circumstances will occasionally warrant the use of assets at other sites. Such circumstances will most often relate to using assets in an activity directly related to one's profession; professor, scholar, activity director, engineer, chairman, etc. However, circumstances may warrant the use of equipment for purely personal reasons. Requests for personal use of assets, on or off site, should be made on a request form designed specifically for

Responsible Person	Responsibility Assigned
All Employees	Custody, maintenance, and reasonable security of all fixed assets purchased for, or assigned to, their respective agency. Proper care and security of any fixed assets that they may use or observe.
Department Head	Custody, maintenance, and reasonable security of all fixed assets purchased for, or assigned to, their respective department.
Custodian	Receipt of the assets under his or her care. Acceptance of overall responsibility for the assets and the use and upkeep of the assets.
Fixed Assets Manager	Seeing that the assets are inventoried, accounted for, and ultimately disposed of according to agency policies and procedures. Maintaining a listing of all fixed assets assigned to the agency, affixing identification tags to new acquisitions, reporting insurable values, and managing the annual inventory control program.

Table 2-1: Responsibility Assignments

that purpose. The personal use of agency assets, even when approved as an exception to general policy, should be for very limited time periods. The public sector agency cannot support the acquisition of assets to support both agency use and at home use. The agency must define its policy on the personal use of agency assets. Additionally, a policy is needed defining the responsibility for the assets whenever losses occur. In those cases where the assets is being used for approved professional purposes, and proper approval has been obtained in advance, the agency should assume responsibility if the assets is lost, stolen, or damaged through no fault or negligence of the user. In those cases where the assets is being used solely for approved personal purposes, even if the user has obtained the approval of the appropriate approval authority, the individual should assume personal responsibility for the assets.

Capitalization Policy

Capitalization refers to the process of assessing assets to determine if the assets has a life expectancy of one year or more and an acquisition cost equal to the capitalization limit or more. Assets such determined are established as an inventoriable asset and the inclusion of the cost of that asset in the agency's balance sheet. Assets is capitalized if it costs over a certain dollar limit, established by the agency, and has a useful life of more than one year. The dollar limit is referred to as the capitalization limit. Assets, when capitalized, is given a permanently assigned identification number and periodically inventoried. The assets must be tracked, accounted for, and disposed of according to agency fixed assets policies and procedures.

The capitalization limit includes freight and the costs to put the asset in service. Items of fixed assets that are components of an asset should be added together before applying the capitalization limit. If a new component extends the useful life of an existing asset, it should be capitalized. However, repair and maintenance costs should not be included.

The establishment of a capitalization limit is the responsibility of the agency. However, the Office of Management and Budget in OMB Circular A-21 and OMB Circular A-110 has set the acquisition costs at $5,000 or more per unit to be considered equipment. The purposes of these constraints are to determine costs applicable to grants, contracts, and other agreements with institutions of higher education, hospitals, and non-profit organizations. Lower limits may be established solely for accountability and tracking purposes. Agencies must be cognizant of these rules in establishing their capitalization limits.

Capitalization is an accounting term and is used by the accounting department. It establishes the dollar limit above which the fixed assets shall be placed on the accounting records. If the capitalization limit is set high, $5,000, for example, and assets below that limit are not tracked, undue losses may occur. Agencies may establish a lower limit than the capitalization limit solely for the purpose of preventing losses from pilferage. This tracking limit should not be set so low that it cost more to track the assets than it does to replace them.

New acquisitions that meet the capitalization limit are to be capitalized per the agency's policies and procedures. Expenditures that increase the future benefits from an existing asset beyond its previously assessed standard of performance are to be capitalized if the cost exceeds the capitalization limit. Increased future benefits typically include:

An extension in the estimated useful life of the asset.

An increase in the capacity of an existing asset.

A substantial improvement in the quality of output or a reduction in previously assessed operating costs.

Capital leases are to be capitalized if the cost equals or exceeds the capitalization limit. Capital leases are leases that transfer substantially all the benefits and risks inherent in the ownership of fixed assets to the public sector agency. A lease should meet one or more of the following four criteria to qualify as a capital lease:

By the end of the lease term, ownership of the leased asset is transferable to the agency; or

The lease contains a bargain purchase option; or

The lease term is 75 percent or more of the estimated useful life of the asset; or

The lease qualifies as a capital lease if, at the inception of the lease, the present value of the minimum lease payments, excluding executory costs, insurance, taxes and maintenance, etc, is 90 percent or more of the fair market value of the asset.

Any donated assets to the agency meeting the capitalization dollar threshold should be capitalized in the same manner as assets obtained through acquisition. The determination of the fair market value of donated assets for Internal Revenue Service (IRS) purposes is the responsibility of the donor. However, the agency must determine the fair market value for the purpose of determining if the capitalization limit has been met. Fair market value means the best estimate of the gross proceeds that would be recovered if the fixed assets were to be sold by competitive bid. If the acquisition cost is known an additional method of determining the fair market value is to use Table 2-2.

Assets, new and used, may be obtained from federal, state or other sources. Fixed assets purchased from such sources should be capitalized in the same manner as new assets obtained through acquisition. However, the agency must determine the fair market value for the purpose of determining if the capitalization limit has been met. Fair market value for such assets can be determined by the use of Table 2-2, if the acquisition cost is known.

Condition	Fair Market Value
New or no repairs necessary	75% of acquisition cost
Used-repairs of 10% or less	50% of acquisition cost
Used-repairs of 11% to 50%	20% of acquisition cost
Used-repairs of 51% to 75%	10% of acquisition cost
Used-spare parts only	5% of acquisition cost

Table 2-2: Fair Market Value Determination

Identification And Tagging

Basic control and identification of an asset is usually accomplished through a serially numbered metal or durable plastic tag affixed to the asset. Identification tags, Figure 2-1, should have a permanent adhesive backing that adheres to all surfaces. Identification tags are also available with bar codes, Figure 2-2. Unless otherwise waived, every capitalized asset must have such an identification tag affixed. Those assets where it is impossible to affix a permanent tag must have a number etched or painted onto it to positively identify the asset as a capitalized asset. Tags should be affixed immediately after the item is acquired. Once applied, care should be taken not to paint over or obliterate the identification number.

Figure 2-1: Metal Identification Tags[4]

Some assets do not lend themselves to tagging, painting, or etching due to the physical characteristics of the asset. In such cases, a number can be assigned to the asset that makes it readily apparent that it is not capable of being tagged. The fixed assets manager must establish a listing of fixed assets numbers to use for this purpose.

Figure 2-2: Bar Coded[5]

All tags or numbers should be uniformly located. When practical, the tag should be placed near the manufacturer's nameplate or as follows:

Desks: Left side of knee space.

Chairs: Middle upper edge of back or inside right rear leg.

File cabinets, racks, etc.: Front top left corner or under manufacturer's nameplate.

Equipment and other furnishing: Where convenient but not distracting from appearance of the asset.

Automotive and other rolling stock: Where easily visible, but not subject to obliteration.

Microcomputers: Rear of the central processing unit (CPU). Identification Tag.

Certain items should not be tagged. Library books, maps, films and non-capitalized leased or rented equipment should not be tagged. Specific exceptions to the established tagging policies and procedures should be defined for all to understand.

Summary

In this chapter, the discussion has primarily centered on the authority for a fixed assets management function, control and accountability for fixed assets, assigning responsibility for fixed assets, and setting the capitalization limits.

To be effective the fixed assets management program must be based on a resolution, charter, specific statutes, or legislation. The authorizing legislation may be very specific as to the fixed assets management methods and restrictive as to the extent of the authority that may be delegated. However, the overall purpose should not be to restrict operations, but to gather and maintain information needed for the preparation of financial statements and to afford control and accountability over assets while preventing loss and abuse. In addition to appropriate legislation supporting the fixed assets management function, there also should be written policies and procedures to govern the day-to-day operations. Policies are considered broad guidelines to activities and to the development of operating procedures. Procedures are the detailed steps to be taken in order to accomplish the job. Procedures answer the "how to" questions. Such questions as, how to identify assets, how to effect the transfer assets and who has responsibility for assets are answered in the fixed assets management operating procedures guide.

Control is called for to detect possible or actual departure from policies and procedures and in the end to allow for effective corrective action. The ten prerequisites of adequate control were introduced as:

Controls must reflect the nature and needs of the activity.

Controls should report deviations promptly.

Controls should be forward looking.

Controls should point up exceptions at critical points.

Controls should be objective.

Controls should be flexible.

Controls should reflect the organizational pattern.

Controls should be economical.

Controls should be understandable.

Controls should lead to corrective action.

Accountability is a key feature of the public sector. The public sector is answerable to the taxpayers such that it must aspire to policies that are compatible with public desires. There is an underlying distrust of the public sector by the people. Therefore, most programs and policies in government contain a high degree of accountability and numerous control programs. Fixed assets management is no exception. The primary purpose for fixed assets management is to ensure accountability of the significant investment in assets entrusted to the public sector administrators.

Public sector personnel at all levels are responsible for the custody, maintenance and reasonable security for all assets purchased for, or assigned to, their respective department or activity. All employees should be concerned with the proper care and security of any assets that they use or observe. Ownership of such assets rests with the federal, state, or local entity. This is true even if the assets are purchased with individual departmental funds or from special equipment appropriations or are acquired by gift, grant or contract.

Capitalization refers to the establishment of an asset as an inventoriable asset and the inclusion of the cost of that asset in the agency's balance sheet. Fixed assets is capitalized if it costs over a certain dollar limit, established by the agency, and has a useful life of more than one year. Such fixed assets is given a permanently assigned identification number and periodically inventoried. The fixed assets must be tracked, accounted for, and disposed of according to agency fixed assets policy and procedures.

Basic control and identification of an asset is usually accomplished through a serially numbered metal or durable plastic tag affixed to the asset. Identification tags should have a permanent adhesive backing that adheres to all surfaces. Unless otherwise waived, every capitalized asset should have an identification tag affixed.

Questions

1. What is the purpose of fixed assets management?
2. List the ten requirement of adequate control.
3. What is accountability use for?
4. Who has responsibility for fixed assets?
5. What is centralized fixed assets management?

6. Describe decentralized fixed assets management.

7. What is capitalization limit?

8. Do all assets lend themselves to being tagged?

Notes

[1] Harold Koontz and Cyril O'Donnell, *Principles of Management: An Analysis of Management Functions*, (McGraw-Hill Book Company, New York, 1972) 586.

[2] Billy E. Goetz, *Management Planning and Control*, (McGraw-Hill Book Company, New York, 1949), 229.

[3] *Performance Measurement Information*, Government Accounting Standards Board of the United States, http://www.rutgers.edu/Accounting/raw/gasb/seagov/accounta.htm.

[4] MetalCraft ID Plates and Label, PO Box 1468, Mason City, IA 50402-1568, http://idplate.com/auograph.htm.

[5] Ibid.

Chapter 3 Inventorying and Reporting

Purpose

The purpose of this chapter is to discuss the inventorying and reporting requisites encountered by the fixed assets manager.

Objectives

Upon completing this chapter, you should be able to:

- Understand why a fixed assets management program is required.

- Describe the fixed assets management cycle.

- Discuss the processes required to perform a physical inventory.

- Differentiate between transfers of fixed assets; lost, missing, and stolen fixed assets; and trade-in of fixed assets.

- Understand the necessity of a fixed assets management inventory system.

- Describe the forms and reports needed to manage fixed assets.

Introduction

The importance of developing and maintaining complete and accurate fixed assets records cannot be emphasized too strongly. In the public sector there is a duty and responsibility to afford protection for assets. This protection is for losses from natural disasters, theft, fire, and an abundance of other ills that can befall a public sector organization. Protection is afforded in the way of insurance on the fixed assets to supply for replacement if damaged or destroyed. Accurate fixed assets records are prerequisites to prove the severity of the losses once they have occurred. The fixed assets management inventory program provides for such an eventuality. Such a program is to supply internal control of assets including proof of existence, ownership, location and proper valuation. Additionally, legislation may call for public entities to be accountable for assets.

An accurate fixed assets management inventory program is essential to meet the growing demands from federal and state-funding sources for improved control and accountability over fixed assets. The importance of accountability over assets assists in the identification of assets for government grants, contracts, and appropriations. In addition, OMB Circular A-110 and other government regulations covering administration of agreements with federal government agencies require that public agencies avoid purchasing "unnecessary or duplicative items."[1] The fixed assets management inventory program is the mainstay for determining what assets are on-hand. Inaccurate records cannot be allowed. There is too much to lose in lost equipment funding from federal grants.

This chapter will address the keeping of the fixed assets records. Subjects to be discussed are: an overview of the fixed assets management inventory program, what assets to track, what data to maintain, how often should fixed assets be inventoried, the importance of a management information system, who should inventory fixed assets and how to account for lost or missing assets. The accuracy of fixed assets records cannot be over-emphasized. Proper communication of asset related activity will ensure maximum accuracy of the fixed assets management inventory program.

Management Inventory Program

The fixed assets management inventory program is necessary to:

Be accountable for all inventoriable assets under control as mandated by agency regulations.

Give internal control of assets including proof of existence, ownership, location and proper valuation.

Present uniform procedures to furnish information for effective analysis and control of expenditures.

The fixed assets management inventory program will make available:

Compliance with public sector agency policies and procedures.

A central fixed assets control system to serve the needs of the agency.

A database of fixed assets information to meet fixed assets management needs and reporting.

Improved fixed assets utilization through control and identification.

A database to meet requirements of risk management and a basis for identifying fixed assets for any self-insurance program.

A basis for project management and to budget future capital replacement requirements.

The fixed assets management inventory program will have the following affect on personnel:

Supply data on fixed assets from a central database.

Entail information on the physical mobility of fixed assets through normal activities (i.e., additions, transfers, retirements and dispositions).

Necessitate participation in an annual inventory to meet agency policies and procedures.

Fixed Assets Management Cycle

The fixed assets management cycle is the cycle of activities from the acquisition of the asset to the final disposition of the assets at the end of their useful life. The cycle is composed of 7 steps:

Acquisition: The cycle begins with the acquisition, purchase, gift or otherwise, of an asset and the determination that the asset is to be capitalized. To be capitalized the asset has to meet the agency's capitalization limit and have a useful life of one year or more.

Receiving: The asset is formally received and accepted by the agency. Receipt may be verified by entry into an automated purchasing system or by hard copy document. In the case of donated fixed assets, receipt can be verified by a letter to the donor.

Payment: Payment is made for the asset according to the terms of the purchase order or recognition of acceptance of a gift made to the donor. The payment includes the acquisition cost, freight and all other costs to put the asset in service. Acquisition cost of donated fixed assets is determined by its fair market value.

Identification: The asset is identified as an asset, tagged or otherwise identified and entered into the fixed assets management inventory system. Assets are identified with a permanently attached identification tag, etching or by painting on the identification number.

Inventory: The longest step in the cycle. The asset is used over its useful life. Assets are inventoried and accounted for during this step until they are no longer needed. The agency's policies and procedures determine the inventory interval.

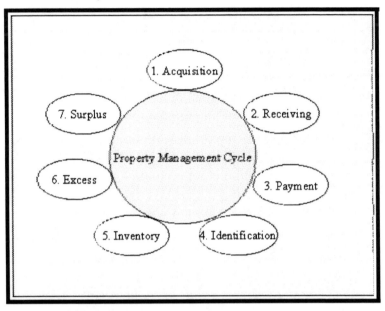

Figure 3-1: Fixed Assets Management Cycle

Excess: The asset is declared as excess to the user's needs. The asset may be transferred to another user where it will continue to be used, accounted for and inventoried. Assets may be declared as excess more than once until the asset is no longer needed.

Surplus: The last step in the fixed assets management cycle. The asset is declared to be surplus property and to have no further value to the agency. The asset is disposed of by sale or discarding depending on the residual value. Sale can be by auction, sealed bid, spot sale, or through a sales store.

Physical Inventories

The physical inventory function is one of the most important functions in the management of fixed assets and the particular inventory verification procedures that are employed are of critical importance to the success of the fixed assets management program. Since the agency cannot use assets that it does not own, failure of the fixed assets management function to maintain an adequate physical inventory has a profound influence over the goals and objectives of the fixed assets management function and the entire agency. Missing assets results in increased agency costs in the form of delayed programs and lost opportunities not to mention lost monies. The purpose of the physical inventory function is to allow for an accurate accounting of owned assets, to guarantee that adequate numbers of assets are maintained and to ensure that assets are maintained in usable condition. If the physical inventory function is not effective, these purposes are not well served.

There is only one means to verify the fixed assets inventory, and that is to physically inventory the assets. Physical inventories are necessary on a regularly scheduled basis. The time intervals vary, some agencies physically inventory their assets every two years; however, the normal inventory interval is one year. The inventory verification may be assigned to the custodian for the assets. The custodian is responsible for the assets and as such is held responsible for the control and accountability of the assets. However, another method of verification is to have an outside party who is neither directly responsible (having custody and receipt/issue authority) for the assets nor supervised by the person responsible for performing the inventory. This last method, when used, ensures completely unbiased inventory verification. There are two ways for scheduling inventory verifications. The first method is to inventory all assets at once (full physical inventory verification). The second method is to perform inventory verifications on a few departments each month (cyclical inventory verification).

The advantages of the full physical inventory verification are:

It is the only means to catch all of the problems at once. This method may be necessary if there are extensive inventory problems.

It accommodates a seasonal agency where there is a slack period at the same time each year when inventory verification can be accomplished without operational interference.

It "gets it all over with" at one time.

It may be the only method authorized by internal and external auditors.

The disadvantages of the full physical inventory verification are:

It is difficult to schedule all departments at the same time each year without some degradation.

There may be an effect on fixed assets management service, since the operation may have to shut down to perform the verification.

If the full physical inventory has to be performed without shutting down operations, the weekend has got to be used and the cost in overtime can outweigh the advantages.

The time and expense to prepare for full physical inventory verification is significant.

The cyclical inventory verification is whereby a certain number of departments are inventoried each month, with the objective of assuring that all departments are inventoried during the year. The number of departments inventoried each month is calculated by dividing the total number of departments by 12. For example, if the number of agency departments is 48, dividing by 12 indicates that 4 departments would be inventoried each month.

The advantages of the cyclical inventory verification method are:

The cyclical inventory verification allows for verification without any major interference to normal operations.

The inventory can be conducted during normal working hours.

There are minimal interruptions in fixed assets management service.

The disadvantages of the cyclical inventory verification method are:

If fixed assets records are not accurate to start with, this method takes a long time to discover all errors and correct them.

Caution should be exercised in scheduling when using either method. Some departments are busier during certain times of the year and should not be scheduled to perform inventory verifications during those times. For example, the athletic department should not be scheduled to perform inventory verifications during football season, additionally; the finance department's inventory verification should not be scheduled during their year-end close out period.

If the physical inventory indicates that there are missing assets, an investigation is vital to determine the circumstances surrounding the loss. An unbiased department within the agency or an outside source can be used to perform the investigation. Public safety offices are well equipped to perform such investigations. A formal written report and a copy of any police investigation report is retained on file in the fixed assets management function. When the value of missing fixed assets is greater than a pre-determined level, fixed assets management should review the inventory with the responsible person and resolve discrepancies.

Most, if not all, physical inventories require that the physical inventory be performed on site. The fixed assets is used and located in the departments away from the centralized fixed assets management department. The fundamental issue is should the physical inventory be centralized within the fixed assets management department or decentralized to the departmental custodian.

The size of the inventory and agency may be determinants in the physical inventory centralization/decentralization issue. If there is a large inventory that is dispersed over a large area that is assigned to many departments, it may be more cost effective and efficient to have the departmental custodians perform the physical inventory. However, if the inventory is relatively small and the agency is centrally located at one place, it may be more appropriate to have the fixed assets management department perform all physical inventories. Understandably, there is no one clear solution to the issue. It is mainly an issue that needs to be analyzed and decision made on the best possible solution for the agency involved.

Another determinant may be the matter of staffing. Centralized physical inventories performed by the fixed assets management department will entail that the fixed assets management department has adequate staff to perform the inventories. A very large inventory will require a large staff to physically inventory the assets on an annual basis. The cost to add sufficient staff may be prohibitive and it may be more efficient to decentralize the physical inventory function. Decentralized physical inventories, on the other hand, will necessitate that the departmental custodians be properly trained to perform the inventory. The time and cost to adequately train the departmental custodians may not be appropriate to the task. A satisfactory training program conducted by the fixed assets management department will be needed and may be an additional burden on the fixed assets management department. Additionally, fixed assets management personnel are not always familiar with the identity and location of assets making it more time consuming on their part to perform the physical inventory. Departmental custodians are more familiar with the assets assigned to their department and may, therefore, be better equipped to locate and inventory the assets.

Fixed Asset Transfers

Transfers between departments will take place during the useful life of assets. The fixed assets manager has got to be able to cope with transfers and not lose track of assets as they are moved from department to department. Use of a transfer form that allows for accountability and assignment of responsibility is typically used to accomplish transfers. The transfer process is needed to relieve the owning custodian of his or her responsibility for assets and assign responsibility to a new custodian. The process involves relieving the owning custodian of responsibility and assigning the responsibility to the new custodian. The process is an approval procedure where the owning custodian approves the transfer to the new custodian and the new custodian accepts responsibility for the asset. Since this is a responsibility assignment the process necessitates approval by both parties. The process also involves the physical movement of the asset between custodians. Assets should not be physically moved until the process has been initiated and approved. Once both parties have approved the transfer the asset can be moved to the new location. Proper tracking and responsibility tend to be lost when assets are physically moved prior to documentation completing the transfer. Accountability remains a prime concern during the transfer process. The transferring custodian, receiving custodian and fixed assets manager have varying responsibilities during the transfer transaction.

The transferring department or custodian is responsible for initiating the process and completion of the necessary fixed assets transfer request. The transferring custodian owns the asset and is the responsible party to gain relief of accountability.

The receiving department or custodian is responsible for accepting responsibility for the asset once the transaction has been completed. The asset is being transferred to the receiving custodian and he or she is required to attest to accept the accountability and responsibility for the asset.

The fixed assets manager is responsible for updating the fixed assets management inventory system with the new custodian and location of the asset.

The computer has significantly improved the proper documenting of transfers. However, the fixed assets management inventory system will only be as accurate as the input data. When transfer data is not input in a accurate and timely manner, the integrity of the fixed assets management program will be suspect and confidence in the program will be lost. Sufficient transfer policies and procedures will significantly increase the accuracy of the transfer process. Custodian training in the proper procedures will assist in the awareness development. The training program should address the transfer procedure and completion of forms.

Lost, Missing Or Stolen Fixed Assets

No matter how good the fixed assets management policies and procedures are, there will be lost assets. Some will just simply be lost or missing due to unknown circumstances while others will be stolen. The physical inventory is the best tool for detecting such losses. However, by the time that the physical inventory is completed, it is normally too late to adequately investigate and locate the asset. The best possible scenario is to minimize losses through positive security measures, unannounced physical inventories and education. Positive security measures are through the use of locks on highly pilferable assets such as videocassette recorders, televisions, computers, and printers. This method is especially effective in laboratories used by a large number of people. Other security measures call for positive identification and signatures such as by a hand receipt to check out and use assets. Unannounced physical inventories can be made by the fixed assets manager when tagging other assets in a department or on a regularly scheduled basis. Agency auditors may be called upon to assist in the process by performing unannounced follow-up inventory verifications.

Trade-In Of Fixed Assets

Occasionally, assets will be used as trade-in credit on the purchase of new assets. Whenever this situation occurs the asset traded has got to be removed from the fixed assets management inventory system. Trade-in transaction should be tracked with care to ensure that the traded asset is properly removed and the new asset is added to the fixed assets management inventory system. This is especially true when using printed documents to record the transaction. The use of printed documents to record the trade-in process may hamper the tracking of the transaction. Users have a tendency to lose interest in completing the documentation after the receipt of the new asset.

Starting the trade-in documentation during the purchasing cycle and notifying the fixed assets manager will ensure the smooth tracking of the transaction. Using assets for trade-in credit is beneficial to the agency and department and should not be degraded due to improper documentation. When trade-in assets are not removed from the fixed assets management inventory system the organization's capitalized assets will be overstated. Accurate financial accounting is dependent upon the fixed assets management program for accurate documentation.

Management Inventory System

The computer and innovations in software systems have revolutionized the fixed assets management function. Only those who remember what it was like to try to operate a fixed asset management function with a manual system can fully appreciate the implication of that statement. However, automated systems have presented fixed assets managers with new and difficult challenges.

Automated systems are so accurate, if data are entered accurately in the beginning, and data are available so quickly that it is next to impossible to not have a good automated system. It doesn't make sense to spend thousands of dollars on new technology just to know what assets are owned. The existence of this new technology demands that we use it to its fullest capabilities. Procedures may be tightened to ensure the accuracy of fixed assets records, the number and types of assets owned and the location of assets. As the accuracy improves it is possible to reduce the number of assets of a particular type, thereby, allowing additional assets of other types to be purchased. Instead of having to maintain two or three assets of a particular type that are only partially used, one asset can be maintained, moved around in the agency and tracked as it is moved. The computer can be used to collect and creatively analyze usage patterns, to produce fixed assets reports and to carry out modeling studies that will lead to further creative means of managing asset usage. Once an automated system is introduced many changes in policies and procedures will be essential. The level of accuracy will demand that fixed assets management activities take place more frequently and in better detail. It is almost impossible to maintain a properly functioning fixed assets management program in today's global world without the aid of an automated system.

Costs for hardware has been declining over the past years. Not only is the cost lower but the capabilities are greater. The typical 1987 model microcomputer had 20 MB of hard drive capacity, 512 KB of RAM and operated at a snail's pace. The cost of such a machine was in excess of $2,500.00 without printer. And printers were a different story altogether. They were slow, low resolution, dot-matrix printers and cost in the neighborhood or $800.00 per printer. The cost of hardware in 1999 has decreased and the capabilities are greater. A typical 1999 model microcomputer has a 10 GB hard drive, 64 to 128 MB of RAM, operates at 450 MHz, has a 17 inch color monitor and cost less than $1,500.00. Printers are faster and have higher resolution. Inkjet and laser printers are in vogue and cost much less than $1,000.00. Expensive mainframe computers have been replaced with more cost efficient minicomputers. No matter, it cost taxpayers dollars to obtain these automated systems and the fixed assets management function may have to cost justify the purchase of an automated system.

Unfortunately, software costs have been increasing as the hardware costs have been declining. However, the good news is that software is plentiful. Fixed assets management readily lends itself to being automated. A fixed assets management inventory system is a matter of accounting for assets by tracking certain data about those assets. These types of transactions are suitable for automation. In many cases software drives the selection of the hardware used by fixed assets management. Whether the software will be installed on a microcomputer, minicomputer or a mainframe computer, whether it will be a stand alone system or distributed process, where it will be located and who will maintain the system are to be determined by the complexity and size of the fixed assets management records to be maintained. Web based systems operating on the World

Wide Web are becoming more available and are desired for their networking capabilities. A complete evaluation of the fixed assets management function and the agency's policies and procedures will be necessary to determine what type of hardware and software to use.

Regardless of the method of automation a fixed assets management inventory system will include provisions for inputting, processing, storing and displaying output in a useful form. The system will include provisions for:

Automatically capturing assets as they are acquired.

Methods for recording cost, location and responsibility assignments.

Historical tracking of acquisitions and disposals.

Report generation of fixed assets records, physical inventories and historical transactions.

Fixed assets management inventory systems will contain data elements to record identification, accounting and ownership of fixed assets. All data elements are not necessarily used but should be available for use. Commercial off-the-shelf fixed assets management inventory system software is delivered with more data elements than are needed. Custom written software is written to only incorporate those data elements that will be used. The selection of custom written software, while adequate for recording purposes, does not stimulate creativity and innovation. What is promoted is the "this is the way we have always done it" attitude. Although this may be adequate, the "old way" of managing fixed assets may not be adequate to comply with new federal, state and local requirements. Suggested data elements are:

Agency Name: The agency name – down to the lowest level that is consistent with ownership of fixed assets.

Account Number: This is the account number in which the asset is being used. This may or may not be the original purchasing account and can be one or more accounts.

Acquisition Method: The method used to acquire the asset. Possible methods are by purchase order, gift, federal, grant, state, etc.

Asset Number: The control number inscribed on, or contained on the asset tag attached or referring to, an asset.

Availability: Whether the asset is available for use.

Commodity Code: The code assigned to an asset that correlates to a descriptive title.

Condition: The condition of the asset.

Costs: A number of costs are used.

Acquisition Cost: The total cost assigned to the asset. Total cost includes cost of freight and the costs to put an asset into service. Repairs and maintenance costs should not be included.

Freight: The cost to ship the asset to the agency, if paid by the agency.

Insurance Cost: The cost to insure the asset.

Taxes: Taxes that the agency is required to pay.

Other Cost: Other cost associated with the acquisition of the asset.

Dates: Various dates should be maintained as follows:

Disposal Date: The date that the agency officially relinquishes responsibility for the asset.

Acquisition Date: The date the agency took title to, or assumes responsibility for, an asset.

Next Inventory: The date that the next inventory is due.

Last Inventory: The date of the last inventory.

Date Tagged: The date that the fixed assets function tagged the asset.

Available Date: The date that the asset will be available for use.

Depreciation: The portion of the cost of fixed assets representing the expiration in service life of the asset attributable to wear and tear, deterioration, action of the physical elements, inadequacy and/or obsolescence which is charged systematically over the useful life of the asset.

Description: Name of the asset. Caution should be used when establishing descriptions especially if the fixed assets system will be used to search on description. Uniform descriptions should be developed and adhered to when entering the fixed assets into the database. For example, an executive desk may be described as Desk, Executive; Executive Desk; Desk, Exec; and so on. The description should be entered in all uppercase or title case format. Regardless of the format selected consistency should be used throughout the system.

Disposal Authorization: To record the authority for disposal of an asset. Specific disposal authority should be assigned to certain individuals within the organization.

How Tagged: The type of tag used to identify the asset. Codes should include painted on, metal tag, or pressure sensitive tag.

Inventory Type: Annual or cyclical inventory.

Location Code: The location code referring to the normal physical location of the asset. Codes should be established that are meaningful without the assistance of a Help function. For example, abbreviate the names of buildings if that is the customary identification used in the agency. Building numbers are meaningless if no one knows the numbers. The effectiveness of using locator codes in this manner will depend on the number of characters available for the code. Location codes may include the following:

Campus Code: (Educational Institutions) The campus or other location where the fixed assets is located.

Building: The building number or abbreviated name where the fixed assets are located.

Room/Floor: The room number and floor where the fixed assets is located.

Department: The owning department code.

Other Location: Other locations not covered above, such as, outside storage, football field, park, etc.

Manufacturer: The name of either the manufacturer or the commonly accepted name, if none, then vendor name.

New/Used: An indication whether the asset was obtained new or used.

Order Number: The number of the purchasing document used for the acquisition of the asset.

Ownership Status: An indication as to possible claims against the asset by outside parties (i.e., federal government, state, etc.).

Quantity: The physical count of the inventoriable items. For equipment, this number should be expressed as whole units.

Salvage Value: The portion of an asset's cost that is recoverable at the end of its service life less any disposal costs.

Serial Number: The sequential identification number assigned by the manufacturer. Do not confuse with the model number.

Useful Life: The estimated useful life of the asset in years.

Voucher Number: The voucher number used to make payment for the asset.

Forms

Although the computer and innovations in software have revolutionized the fixed assets management function, certain activities are still completed by the use of printed forms. Forms are needed to establish control and accountability over assets. Typically, forms have been printed documents that are manually transferred between fixed assets management and the various agency departments.

Nobody knows who invented the first form (he or she must have been a bureaucrat, though) but they've been proliferating like weeds ever since. There's good reason for this: they're useful. In a society like ours, which depends so heavily on the processing of information, they're essential for organizing both the way the information is gathered and how it's presented. If a census-taker merely asks a person to "tell me all about your household," she'll probably get some of the data she's after, but she'll miss at least some, and receive unwanted information. In this disorganized state, the information is almost useless. But give the same census-taker a form to guide the data collection, and life suddenly becomes much easier.

Because you intend for your forms to gather information, you have to persuade people to fill them out. Almost on principle, people dislike forms, and if the form is badly organized, too long, and filled with irrelevant questions, nobody will touch it. The following are a few things you can do to create user-friendly forms:[2]

If you can, create an enticement to complete the form.

Keep the length of the form short.

Briefly tell the reader why you want the data and how it is to be used.

Ask general questions first, starting with a couple of easy ones and then go for the detail.

Nobody reads forms carefully, so ask your questions as briefly and clearly as you can.

Avoid ambiguous questions, such as, "Do you find our service good?"

Avoid leading questions, where the wording influences the answer.

Before putting the form into service, test it on some real live people and use the feedback to modify it.

Printed forms supply a written record of all transactions related to an asset and are used to substantiate accountability. However, there are certain disadvantages to using printed forms. Printed forms are manually completed and distributed. Forms distributed by manually means tend to get lost in the distribution channels. To be effective printed forms have got to be kept on file, which means that they have to be stored in a suitable filing medium such as a filing cabinet. When filed a filing system is necessary for later retrieval. These processes are labor intensive and, therefore, expensive to use. New managers or others working in the fixed assets management function may not understand a filing system developed by another manager.

An alternative to printed forms is the use of World Wide Web (Web) forms. The Web is providing many innovations with the use of Web forms. Web forms can be used to gather the same information that is gathered with printed forms. Once completed the data can be saved in a database on a server allowing for later retrieval and manipulation, a feature that makes Web forms very beneficial to fixed assets management. Web forms contain the data elements, a Submit button that is used to send the data to a server and a Clear button to remove existing entries from the fields. The most significant advantage of Web forms over printed forms is the distribution process. Once completed, the Web form can be distributed electronically between the custodian, fixed assets manager, department heads and others, as needed. Manual filing systems are not needed and all authorized users may be granted access to the forms over the organization's network.

Fixed assets management uses five forms to collect the necessary data to management the function. The identification and accountability process starts with the completion of the Fixed Assets Receipt and ends with the Surplus Declaration Form. Fixed assets management forms have different purposes and uses:

Fixed Assets Receipt: The Fixed Assets Receipt is the primary form used to identify as asset as property and establish accountability. It is usually printed from the fixed assets management inventory system and includes preliminary identification data, such as: acquisition costs, acquisition date, account numbers used to purchase the fixed assets, description of the fixed assets and so forth. The fixed assets manager uses the Fixed Assets Receipt when tagging the property and usually assigns the property or asset number and completes the location data. Since the Fixed Assets Receipt is the primary document used to establish accountability it is by far the most important fixed assets management form. Once completed the Fixed Assets Receipt should be retained on file in the fixed assets management office for the life of the asset plus one-year, as a minimum.

Fixed Assets Transaction Request: The Fixed Assets Transaction Request is a multipurpose form used to transfer property within the agency and declare property as excess and surplus. It is a very valuable form to the fixed assets management function because it is used to transfer accountability. If the form is not effectively used the integrity of the fixed assets management function will be compromised. The form contains all the necessary information for updating the fixed assets management inventory system. Once completed the Fixed Assets Transaction Request should be maintained on file in the fixed assets management office for the life of the asset.

Personal Use of Fixed Assets Request: Property is intended for use primarily at the designated workplace within the agency, however, certain circumstances will occasionally warrant the personal use of property outside the workplace. Whenever the personal use of property is requested, appropriate authority within the agency must grant approval. The Personal Use of Fixed Assets Request is used to document the approval(s) and to grant authority for an individual to remove the fixed assets from the workplace and to track its location. Personal Use of Fixed Assets Request should be maintained on file in the fixed assets management office for the duration of the loan and one-year afterwards.

Donated Fixed Assets Receipt: The Donated Fixed Assets Receipt is used to record and report the receipt of all donated property regardless of the dollar value. Reporting the receipt of all donated property assists in the determination of whether or not to track the property in the fixed assets management inventory system. The fixed assets manager, also, uses this form much like the Fixed Assets Receipt to identify and assign responsibility for the property. Those assets not meeting the capitalization criteria are not tracked but the form is used to inform upper management of the receipt of the property so that informed decisions on the proper use of the property can be made. Donated Fixed Assets Receipts should be maintained on file in the fixed assets management office for the life of the asset.

Overdue Inventory Verification Notification: The Overdue Inventory Verification Notification is used to notify a department that their inventory verification has not been completed in the time allotted and that the inventory verification is overdue. Departments are asked to complete the form indicating when they expect to complete the inventory verification, request a new Inventory Verification Report, or request a change in the inventory schedule for the department. The Overdue Inventory Verification Notification should be maintained in the fixed assets management office for a period of five years to determine if adjustments to the schedule are needed. Departments that consistently miss the completion dates should be consulted to determine if another inventory time is more appropriate.

Reports

Automated fixed assets management inventory systems are beneficial when producing reports to be used in the management of the fixed assets management function. The system is a giant database containing all of the necessary data to produce meaningful property reports needed to operate the fixed assets management function.

Computers perform four basic tasks that are meaningful to the fixed assets management function. They accept input of data, process the data, store the data and produce output. Previous discussions have principally addressed the inputting, processing and storing of fixed assets management data. Those functions are essential for the proper operation of the fixed assets management program. The accuracy of the input data is the key to successful operations. "Garbage in, garbage out" is a well-known axiom in computer circles. The accuracy of the input task has a direct effect on the output utility. The output is no better than the input data. Reporting is the outcome of the input role. Reports can be produced on the computer monitor or screen and in printed fashion. To produce useful screen reports that all custodians or users can access and use necessitates that the fixed assets management inventory system be networked. Screen reports call for all custodians or users be networked to a central server. The most commonly used output is the printed report. It has traditionally been used to make available the information needed to operate the fixed assets management program and is familiar to all users. Printing a report is the final output result of the fixed assets management inventory system. Most custodians and users more easily understand printed reports. Reports can be rows and columns of information. Users, custodians in particular, have needs for well-developed reports that offer meaningful, useful information as well as look good. Reports, therefore, have to be functionally correct as well as cleverly formatted. Data can be manipulated to supply two report formats:

Columnar Report: A report where the information is displayed vertically with one record per page.

Tabular Report: A report where the rows of records go across the page similar to a spreadsheet and displayed horizontally. Tabular reports are usually multicolumnar reports where the text flows across the page. The tabular report is the most commonly used report format for fixed assets management reports.

Two fixed assets management reports, Departmental Fixed Assets Report and Inventory Verification Report, are the primary reports used. The Departmental Fixed Assets Report gives a listing of all the property owned by a department. It is not needed if the fixed assets management inventory system is networked and custodians have access to their property records. The Inventory Verification Report is the report used in the physical inventory process. The two fixed assets management reports are:

Departmental Fixed Assets Report: This report contains all of the assets owned by a certain custodian or department. It is sorted by property or asset number and contains primarily asset identification and location information. The only cost data is the total acquisition cost. The custodian uses the report to keep abreast of changes in his or her assigned property.

Inventory Verification Report: The Inventory Verification Report is the report used to perform the inventory verification. It contains enough data to locate and identify the asset. A block is available for the custodian to acknowledge the verification.

Summary

This chapter has addressed the actual keeping of inventory records. Subjects discussed were: an overview of the fixed assets management inventory program, what assets to track, what data to maintain, how often should property be inventoried, who should inventory property and how to account for lost or missing assets.

The fixed assets management inventory program is necessary to:

Be accountable for all property under control as mandated by agency regulations.

Allow for internal control of assets including proof of existence, ownership, location and proper valuation.

Make available uniform procedures to furnish information for effective analysis and control of expenditures.

The fixed assets management cycle is the cycle of activities from the acquisition of the asset to the final disposition of the assets at the end of their useful life. The cycle is composed of 7 steps: Acquisition, Receiving, Payment, Identification, Inventory, Excess and Surplus.

The physical inventory function is one of the most important functions in the agency, and the particular inventory verification procedures that are employed are of critical importance to the success of the fixed assets management program. Since the agency cannot use assets that it does not own, failure of the fixed assets management function to maintain an adequate physical inventory has a profound influence over the goals and objectives of the fixed assets management function and the entire agency. Missing assets results in increased agency costs in the form of delayed programs and lost opportunities not to mention lost monies. The purpose of the physical inventory function is to allow for an accurate accounting of owned assets, to ensure that adequate numbers of assets are maintained and to ensure that assets are maintained in usable condition. If the physical inventory function is not effective, these purposes are not well served.

There are two ways of scheduling inventory verifications. The first method is to inventory all assets at once (full physical inventory verification). The second method is to perform inventory verifications on a few departments each month (cyclical inventory verification).

Transfers between departments will take place as time goes on and the fixed assets manager must be able to cope with the situation and not lose track of assets as they are moved from department to department. Assets should not be physically moved until all needed forms have been initiated and approved. Once the transfer has been approved the asset can be moved to the new location. The transferring department or custodian is the responsible agency for completing the fixed assets transfer request. The receiving department or custodian is responsible for accepting responsibility for the asset once the transaction has been completed. The fixed assets manager is responsible for updating the fixed assets management inventory system with the new custodian and location of the asset.

No matter how good the fixed assets management policies and procedures are, there will be lost assets. Some will just simply be lost due to unknown circumstances while others will be stolen. The physical inventory is the best tool for detecting such losses. However, by the time that the physical inventory is completed, it is normally too late to adequately investigate and locate the asset. The best possible scenario is to minimize losses through positive security measures, unannounced physical inventories and education.

Occasionally, assets will be used as trade-in credit on the purchase of new assets. Whenever this situation occurs the asset traded must be removed from the fixed assets management inventory system. Trade-in transaction must be tracked with care to ensure that the traded asset is properly removed and the new asset is added to the fixed assets management inventory system. This is especially true when using printed documents to record the transaction

The fixed assets management inventory system is necessary to account for all fixed assets under the agency's control as mandated by agency regulations, to afford internal control of assets including proof of existence, ownership, location and proper valuation, and to offer uniform procedures to furnish for effective analysis and control of expenditures. Public sector agencies must accurately maintain a fixed assets management inventory system that includes records for all inventoriable assets.

Questions

1. Why is a fixed assets management inventory needed?

2. What are the seven steps in the fixed assets management cycle?

3. Describe the two methods of performing fixed assets inventories.

4. Explain the process of transferring assets.

5. Who should investigate lost, missing, or stolen fixed assets reports?

6. Under what circumstances should fixed assets be used as trade-in credit?

7. What are the provisions for a fixed assets management inventory system?

8. What forms and reports are used to report fixed assets management transactions?

Notes

[1] OMB Circular A-110 (Revised 11/19/93, As Further Amended 8/29/97), *Uniform Administrative Requirements for Grants and Agreements With Institutions of Higher Education, Hospitals, and Other Non-Profit Organizations*, (Office of Management and Budget, Washington, DC, 1993).

[2] Dennis Jones and Neil Randall, *Using Microsoft® FrontPage 98*, (Que Corporation, Indianapolis, IN, 1997), 233.

Chapter 4 Disposition Of Fixed Assets

Purpose

The purpose of this chapter is to outline the disposition of property after it has reached the end of its useful life and is no longer needed by the public sector.

Objectives

Upon completing this chapter, you will be able to:

- Briefly describe the surplus property management principles.

- Explain the surplus property classifications.

- Understand the disposal methods.

- Comprehend the rationalization for selling or not selling surplus property to agency employees.

- Have a handle on the distribution of proceeds form sales of surplus property.

- Describe the many hazardous materials found in the public sector.

Introduction

The last step in the Fixed Assets Management Cycle is to surplus or dispose of assets. At this point is the life cycle of an asset it has finally reached the end of its useful life and has to be disposed of in some manner. The mission of the disposal function is to receive, warehouse and dispose of the agency's surplus property in the best interest of the agency. The central warehousing of surplus property will allow all agency departments one location to acquire needed assets which otherwise might escape the system and be sold to the public. The purposes of the disposal program are:

Elimination of costs related to the warehousing, insurance and accounting systems necessary to fulfill the agency's surplus property responsibility.

Maximize the proceeds by disposing of assets as soon as possible after it becomes excess to an agency's needs.

Establishment of priorities in the disposal process that encourages keeping assets in public use as long as possible.

Conversion of unneeded assets into available funds on a timely basis for offsetting the cost of new assets.

Most property, even thought it has reached or exceeded its useful life, may have some residual value. The Federal government recognized this many years ago and operates one of the most advanced property disposal functions in the world. Like some state governments, the federal government releases certain excess property through intergovernmental programs. Under direction of the General Services Administration, federal surplus property is allocated to several agencies in each state, one of which has a general responsibility and is designated by the state as the federal surplus agency. The state agency, in turn, distributes the assets to eligible recipients. Allocations of federal property to states are made in terms of need, population, per capita income, and other factors. Eligible recipients in the state consist of all public agencies together with not-for-profit enterprises engaged in educational and health programs. States with well-developed programs have inspectors to screen items regularly at military posts and other federal installations and operate trailer-tractor trucks to transport usable items to one or more warehouses located strategically in the state where donees can inspect and acquire them. The federal surplus agency is responsible for redistributing the property in a fair and equitable manner to eligible participants throughout the state.[1] The federal government, as can be seen, recognizes that surplus property has value and considers redistribution as a method of disposing of their surplus property.

Most state and local agencies also operate surplus property programs to dispose of surplus property. The State of South Carolina operates an extensive disposal program. All assets owned by state agencies are considered state property and are reported to the Surplus Property Management Office (SPMO) at the end of their useful life. The SPMO redistributes excess property to other state agencies and disposes of all surplus assets acquired from state agencies at its central facility in Columbia, South Carolina through auction and spot sale.

It is obvious that public sector surplus property has value. The axiom that "One person's junk is another's treasure" really has meaning in the public sector. Surplus public property is made up of every item imaginable from minor supplies to heavy equipment costing in the millions of dollars. It is, therefore, worthy of managing the disposal of such assets to realize the maximum return to the public sector. Without proper management the public sector loses many valuable dollars that could be used to fund other purchases of assets.

Some assets may become more of a burden to dispose of than the overall worth of the property. For example, the cost to dispose of 450-student desks may certainly exceed any value that can be realized from disposing of them. Problems such as this are not uncommon and should be dealt with appropriately. Fixed assets management must have the necessary authority to determine the proper method of disposal even if that method is to donate the property to a worthy organization.

Although surplus property has reached its useful life it may still have value. Because it has value, and value means monetary value in this case, it calls for management to ensure that its value is not lost. It is necessary that property be adequately classified. The classifications will significantly assist in determining the disposal method to use. Excess implies that the property can be further used within the agency while surplus means the property has no further value to the agency and may be disposed of through proper channels. The disposal method will determine what steps to be taken in the disposal process and how much money will be realized from the disposal. The strategy is to select the method that maximizes the return on the assets. The funds realized from sales might represent a signification source of funds to the agency and policies are needed to ensure the funds are used for the best overall purpose. Furthermore, environmental issues have to be faced and compliance with federal, state, and local laws and ordinances have to be ensured. Of major importance, also, is the proper disposal of hazardous materials.

In this chapter surplus property management principles will be developed, surplus property classifications will be defined and disposal methods will be presented. Additionally, the matter of how the agency should distribute the funds realized from surplus property sales will be explored. The importance of recycling, environmental issues and how usable materials can be returned to the manufacturing stream to offset the use of natural resources cannot be overlooked. More and more hazardous materials are showing up in public sector operations. When they become obsolete or of no further value they have to be properly disposed of to ensure compliance with disposal ordinances.

Surplus Property Management Principles

There are certain surplus property management principles that can be used as a guide in the efficient disposal of surplus property. While these principles may not be all encompassing they will assist the fixed assets management function is making sound decisions regarding disposal of surplus property. The surplus property management principles are:

All excess and surplus materials must be considered for disposal: Property is usually thought of as those assets that have been capitalized and are being tracked for accountability. However, there are other items that must be considered for disposal through the fixed assets management program. Obsolete supplies from the stores function, chairs, desks and almost any items that may have some residual value. For example, do not overlook the value of a box of excess computer printer ribbons. They may surely have value and the agency needs to treat their disposal appropriately.

If someone wants it, it has value: There will be many inquiries regarding how to obtain certain surplus property items for personal use. Whenever this occurs it is revealing that the property has some value. Evaluate the inquiry for validity and proceed accordingly.

Maximize the sale of surplus property: Selecting the proper disposal method will ensure that the maximum return for surplus property will be realized. The marketplace must the surveyed to determine what will sell and how to effectively dispose of the surplus property.

Surplus Property Classifications

Surplus property is defined, as property not needed within the agency. Certain surplus property may begin as surplus property but revolve into another classification. For example, property may be classified as redistribution property if efforts to dispose of it as surplus property have failed. Additionally, excess property may revert to being surplus property and put up for sale if the assets cannot be redistributed within the agency. Surplus property is categorized into five classifications:

Surplus Property: Property that is surplus is no longer needed within the agency and includes all excess assets and materials other than items that would be typically disposed of in a wastebasket, such as scrap paper. By far, this includes the greatest proportion of the assets to be disposed of within an agency. This classification may be comprised of excess or obsolete supplies from the stores function to major equipment items. Disposing of assets within this classification will necessitate the maximum amount of time, management and effort in the disposition process. These assets invariably have value on the open market and all efforts to take advantage of obtaining this value for the agency should be explored. Disposal methods may include auction, sealed bid, spot sale and if all else fails donation to a worthy organization.

Excess Property: Excess property is no longer needed by the custodial department but may be used by another department within the agency. This classification includes such items as chairs, desks, vehicles, test equipment office machines, computers, etc. Reuse of excess property should be considered prior to purchase of new items. As a means of making this classification more susceptible to reuse the agency may consider refinishing or reupholstering the items. The federal government and many states operate a prison industry function where such property may be inexpensively refinished or reupholstered. This disposal method includes redistribution; however, excess property may eventually be classified as surplus property where it would be disposed of by auction, sealed bid, spot sale, or if all else fails, donation to a worthy organization.

Scrap: Surplus material, such as metal pieces, broken component parts or inoperable equipment, which has no utility value in its present state. The engineering or physical plant department is a potential source for scrap materials. Metal scraps from large jobs, brass values, copper wire and a multitude of other such items exist in the typical public sector agency. Scrap may be disposed of by sale to a scrap dealer who specializes in buying scrap.

Redistribution: Excess and surplus property may be classified for redistribution within and outside the agency. Certain items, such as mattresses, may not be sold due to local restrictions on the resale of these items. The best value may be realized in this manner by offsetting the costs of disposing of the items in a landfill. Additionally, if the property cannot be redistributed within the agency, it can be considered for redistribution in the local area or donated to worthy organizations such as the Salvation Army or other such organizations. This is not only a very good use of the items but will create goodwill within the local area. The disposal method for this classification is redistribution.

Recyclable: The federal government and most states have recycling programs aimed at reducing the input to landfills and reducing the use of scarce natural resources. This classification includes paper, plastic, aluminum, glass, tin, cloth and used motor oil. Paper includes newsprint, magazines, cardboard, and printing paper. Scrap may include some recyclable materials such as copper wire. The proper classification is unimportant in those cases. It is the overall intent to return the materials to use that is important. Although the dollar return on recyclables is not always that big it is of superior concern that we preserve our scarce natural resources.

Disposal Methods

After determining that the property is surplus to the needs of the agency, the determination of the best disposal method is necessary. The best method is the one that maximizes the return to the agency or in the case of recyclables the method that returns the materials to use while preserving our natural resources. Careful review and analysis of the items to be disposed of and the determination of the method of disposal is paramount to a successful disposal program.

Regardless of the disposal method it has to be made clear that the items are being disposed of "As is, Where is." This translates to mean that the buyer accepts the risk that the items may or may not operate and that the buyer will remove the items from the agency. A Bill of Sale enumerating all conditions of the sale is a technique that can be used to document the transaction. When used both parties, fixed assets management and the buyer should authenticate the Bill of Sale. Duplicate Bills of Sale should be kept on file in the fixed assets management office for three years from the sale.

Payment for the assets is a vital part of the disposal process. There are five payments instruments that can be used to receive payment for the assets.

Personal Checks: Personal checks contain a certain amount of risk for the agency. Checks may be fraudulent or do not have sufficient funds to cover the purchase. Acceptance of personal checks should be made only after obtaining proper identification.

Certified Checks: Certified checks are a safe instrument to accept as payment. They have been paid for in advance and are backed by the issuing institution.

Money Orders: Money orders are in the same category as certified checks. Money orders are a safe instrument to receive as payment. They have been paid for in advance and are backed by the issuing institution.

Credit Cards: Credit cards are another safe instrument to accept. However, credit cards involve paying the credit card company a fee to use their card as payment. The cost range from a low of 3% and upwards of the sale price. Additionally, it may be necessary to sign agreements with more than one credit card company. Credit cards do not contain the risks of fraud, as the credit card issuer is liable.

Cash: Cash is always a payment consideration. However, cash management procedures may be needed. Close accountability for the cash received should be instituted using Bill of Sales or other sales records to substantiate the amount of cash received.

The disposal of surplus property is accomplished by one of seven methods as depicted in Figure 4-1: auction, sealed bids, spot sale, trade-in, redistribution, discard and recycling. Disposal through auction or sealed bid demand that advance notice be given prior to the sale. Advance notice will notify the potential buyers of the impending sale and make available all of the information needed for them to may a decision to participate. Minimum information to include in the advance notice is:

Time and place for the sale for auctions.

Terms and conditions of the sale.

Opening date, time and place for sealed bids.

A newspaper or other media with widespread circulation should be used to advertise the sale. Potential buyers need enough time to schedule their attendance at the auction or to obtain and respond to the sealed bid.

The disposal methods are:

Auction: Auction is a popular disposal method for such items as vehicles, heavy equipment, antiques, and livestock. Auctions are interesting people events. The chants of the auctioneer increase the interest of those in attendance and ensure maximum involvement. It is easy to get caught up in the auction process and catch the auction fever. The auction disposal method will afford the maximum return to the agency in almost all occasions. Auctioning is not without its dangers, however. Unless a bottom acceptable bid is established items may be sold at low prices. Additionally, bidders may get confused at the rapid pace of the auction and bid on items they did not intend to causing a negative opinion of the agency. To be effective, there ought to be a sufficient quantity and variety of property to attract a crowd. The goal is to sell all items. Items not sold are a further burden and cost on the agency. The careful selection of the auctioneer is an important aspect of this method. The auctioneer ought to possess a high degree of integrity and conduct business so as to avoid conflicts with the public. They have to endeavor to keep abreast of market conditions and be informed of federal, state and local laws related to auctions to impart intelligent advice and service. It is highly recommended that auctioneers be members of a national auctioning association.

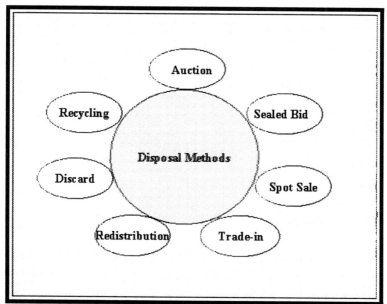

Figure 4-1: Disposal Methods

Sealed Bid: The second disposal method is by sealed bid. This method is used when there is not a large quantity of disposal items and disposal by auction would not be practical. The sale items can be sold individually or grouped into lots of similar items where practical. Grouping items into lots will decrease the overall number of items for sale and vastly assist in the subsequent evaluation of bids received. A Notice of Sale is used as the bidding document. The Notice of Sale will list the supplies or assets being offered for sale and instructions to bidders including the place, date and time set for bid opening. Once received the bids should be secured until opening. A public opening will ensure the integrity of the disposal process. Award is to be made to the highest responsive and responsible bidder provided that the fixed assets manager deems the price offered reasonable. When the price is determined to be unreasonable, the bids may be rejected in whole, or in part, and the sale negotiated beginning with the highest bidder if the negotiated sale price is higher than the highest responsive and responsible bid. In the event of a tie bid the flip of a coin or the draw of a card may determine the award. The bidders have got to be present for the determination. The specifications for the bid ought to be prepared to adequately describe the assets for sale. Some may simply be identified by a brief one or two word description while others may involve a more detailed description. Fixed assets sold shall be paid for within a period specified in the Notice of Sale.

Spot Sale: Spot sale involves pricing items for sale and offering them for sale in a sales mart environment. This method is favored whenever there is a steady supply of items that do not lend themselves to sale by auction or sealed bid. This method calls for a suitable retail sales area and knowledge of retail sales procedures. Using this method eliminates or reduces the requirement for long-term storage of items before sale. Additionally, this method entails close monitoring of pricing policies and procedures to ensure that prices are established fairly while ensuring maximum return to the agency. Prices established based on current market conditions are the best alternative and the fairest to all parties. Prices may be established for all typical items offered and approved by proper authority. One method is to pre-establish a price list for typical sale items. The price list when approved by upper management creates integrity for the price list. Table 4-1 presents a range of prices that can be established for certain common surplus items for sale in a sale mart.

Trade-In: Disposal of surplus property through trade-in is another option that can be considered for those items where the purchase of new items is being considered. Trade-in offers a quick and easy method of disposal. Do not overlook the potential in classifying surplus property as trade-in. If new equipment is being purchased, this method offers a quick and easy means for disposal of the property and possibly saving funds in the process. The need to store the items is eliminated or significantly reduced and the expense of disposing of the item by another means is eliminated. Many times vendors may not want the old items but will offer a trade-in allowance to be competitive. And if the purchase is being made by competitive means, it ensures that the allowance received is a fair price in the marketplace. Therefore, use this method as much as possible as it will return savings in storage, administrative costs and labor. Close coordination between fixed assets management and purchasing is needed to maximize the full potential of the trade-in disposal method.

Item	Item
Desk, Metal (newer) $80.00 - $45 (no return)	Desk, Metal (newer) $85.00 - $50.00 (with return
Desk, Metal (WWII era) $20.00	Desk, Wooden $70.00 - $90.00 (no return)
Desk, Wooden $75.00 - $90.00 (with return)	Cabinet, File, Vertical, 5 drawer $35.00 - $70.00
Cabinet, File, Lateral, 5 drawer $55.00 - $100.00	Bookshelf, Metal $10.00 - $15.00
Bookshelf, Wooden $30.00 - $40.00	Chair, Secretary (no arms) $12.00 - $22.00
Chair, Secretary (with arms) $15.00 - $25.00	Chair, Straight, Metal (no arms) $5.00
Chair, Straight, Metal (with arms) $8.00	Chair, Straight, Wood (no arms) $$10.00 - $15.00
Chair, Straight, Wood (with arms) $15.00 - $20.00	Tablet Armchair $5.00
Table, Wood $25.00 - $40.00	Table, Metal $20.00 - $25.00
Table, Drafting $10.00 - $15.00	Table, End $5.00 - $15.00
Sofa $15.00 - $45.00	Love Seat $10.00 - $35.00
Recliner $20.00 - $35.00	Chalkboard $9.00 - $25.00

Table 4-1: Sale Price Ranges

Redistribution: Redistribution includes the redistribution of excess fixed assets within and outside the agency. The consideration is for redistribution to another department within the agency. If there are no internal requirements, redistribution outside the agency can be considered as a viable disposal method. Other governmental agencies within the local area or elsewhere that have a need for the asset are possible recipients. The South Carolina Consolidated Procurement Code defines the primary role of its Surplus Property Management Office (SPMO) to be redistribution of surplus property and defines the recipients as follows: "The primary role of SPMO shall be to relocate surplus property to eligible governmental bodies, political subdivisions and nonprofit health and educational institutions. The Manager of Supply and Surplus Property Management shall be responsible for determining an applicant's eligibility prior to any transfer of property. The term governmental bodies means any State government department, commission, council, board, bureau, committee, institution, college, university, technical school, legislative body, agency government corporation, or other establishment or official of the executive, judicial, or legislative branches of the State. Governmental body excludes the General Assembly and all local political subdivisions such as counties, municipalities, school districts or public service or special purpose districts. The term political subdivisions includes counties, municipalities, school districts or public service or special purpose districts. The term eligible nonprofit health or educational institutions means tax-exempt entities, duly incorporated as such by the State. The SPMO will maintain sufficient records to support the eligibility status of these entities."

Redistribution brings up the subject of compensation for the redistributed assets. Redistribution within the agency should be at no cost to the receiving department. The assets were initially paid for with agency funds and the assets are still to be used within the agency. However, when redistribution is to outside agencies there needs to be written policy on how to redistribute the funds received for the sale. The redistributing agency expended funds to purchase and maintain the asset and will incur some expenses to store and advertise the asset as being available. One scheme for computing the redistribution fees to outside agencies is:

Vehicles: The NADA loan value shall be used for the sale price. In certain instances, the most recent public sale figures and negotiation with the receiving agency shall be the basis for the sale price.

Boats, Motors, Heavy/Farm Equipment, Airplanes and Other Items With Acquisition Cost Over $5,000: The sale price shall be set from the most recent public sale figures and/or any other method necessary to establish a reasonable value including negotiation with the receiving agency.

Miscellaneous Items With an Acquisition Cost Under $5,000: Use Table 2-2 to compute the fair market value and further negotiate with the receiving agency.

Office Furniture: Use Table 4-1 to compute the sales price.

Discard: If one or more of the above disposal methods fail to present a satisfactory disposal, discard may be considered. However, discard should be the last resort in the disposal process because it cost the disposing agency to use this method. Costs include the cost of the item, carrying costs, dumpster costs and landfill charges. It may be considered more advantageous to the agency to accept a lower than expected sales price for the asset than to pay the additional cost of discarding of the items. Therefore, a careful comparison of all discard costs and a low sale price has got to be made prior to passing up a low sales price for an asset. It may very well be that the discard costs will be in excess to the low sales price. Donation to non-profit organizations such as the Salvation Army may be considered whenever all other means have failed. Donation will save the carrying costs, dumpster costs and landfill charges. Due to the large number of recipients of discarded property qualified organizations should be pre-qualified and approved to receive the discarded property prior to donation to ensure the integrity of the program.

Recycling: Recycling is a technology that transforms discarded materials into useful products. It involves the collection of recyclable materials from the public as well as businesses and industries through a variety of recycling opportunities. After collection these materials have to be processed or prepared to specifications to meet market requirements. We call this stage of processing and brokering the secondary markets stage. Following the secondary market stage, the materials move on to the manufacturer or end user where they are used as raw materials to produce new products. Or, the manufacturer may further process the materials before making the end product.[2]

Recycling will not, in all probably, bring in large sums of funds. For example, right now, the going rate for old newspapers is about $50 a ton and ordinary cardboard boxes that have been flattened are bringing approximately $75 per ton.[3] This will only change if the demand for recycled products rise to the point that it is lucrative to produce recycled products. The prime recycling consideration is to help preserve our natural resources. Again, this will not be accomplished until the demand for recycled products rise. Federal and state governments have established conservation programs that involve the use of recycled products. The Federal Resource

Conservation and Recovery Act of 1976 call for federal agencies to develop affirmative procurement programs for products made with recycled materials. All states and the District of Columbia have programs favoring the use of recycled products. Price preferences for recycled products are in effect in many states providing a 5 to 10% preference for recycled products. But the environmental issues seem to outweigh the negative cost effects at this time. Another consideration are mandated laws dictating that public sector agencies participate in recycling programs, the collection of recyclables and the purchase of recycled product.

Items that can be recycled are:

Batteries: Batteries include nickel-cadmium batteries contained in power tools and telephones and lead acid batteries from vehicles. These items contain hazardous materials and should be handled with care. Most states prohibit the disposal of these batteries in landfills. They contain materials that can be recycled and, therefore, should be recycled.

Plastic: Most plastic can be recycled. The hurdle that has to be faced in plastic recycling is that plastic types not be mixed for recycling. To make matters worse, it is almost impossible to tell one type of plastic from another by sight or touch. The most popular plastic to recycle is plastic containers such as found in milk, water containers and soda bottles. These plastic containers are marked with a large recycling code molded into the plastic on the bottom.

Paper: The majority of paper types can be recycled. Chief among the types of paper found in public agencies is corrugated cardboard, newsprint, phone books, and white office paper. All of these papers may be recycled if handled properly. Newsprint is commonly available, of homogeneous uniformity and easy to recycle. White office paper is the highest grade of paper making it an excellent candidate for recycling. Some paper types cannot be recycled. These include: food contaminated paper, waxed paper, oil soaked paper, carbon paper, thermal fax paper, juice boxes and any paper containing plastic layers or laminations. The paper-recycling objective is to collect large quantities of clean, uncontaminated, dry paper. The paper types have to be sorted and not intermixed to obtain the best return. Collection containers can be easily placed in all offices and other places where paper is used. In some cases, separate containers may be used to sort the paper into the different categories prior to pickup.

Glass: Glass is easy to recognize for recycling. Clear glass is the most valuable for recycling. Broken glass is difficult to sort and makes the recycling process less advantageous. Mixed colored glass has less value. The commingling of glass types will reduce the return. Therefore, do not mix window glass, light bulbs, and mirrors with glass bottles.

Aluminum Cans: Aluminum cans are readily available, easy to collect and recycle centers are available. Aluminum cans contain a recycling symbol that makes it easy to identify them as recyclable. Collection containers can be placed throughout the agency.

Used Motor Oil: Used motor oil is considered hazardous because of the heavy metals and other toxins it contains. Recycling used motor oil is easy. It can be centrally collected in motor pools or at collection points throughout the agency. Specialized companies that specialize in collecting used motor oil for a charge are available for pick up and recycling of the used motor oil. It may be necessary to use such a company because of the hazardous nature of the oil. Used motor oil is also being burned in steam producing boilers and electric generating facilities to produce energy.

Sales To Employees

Should employees be allowed to purchase surplus property? There are two schools of thought on this subject. One school of thought is that since the employees are the ones who decide what and when to declare an item surplus they should not be allowed to purchase. The other school of thought is that if the items are being disposed of by auction or sealed bid, why disallow them from participating. Each school has its strong points; however, there is not a universal consensus. It would appear that there are no drawbacks in allowing employees to bid at auction or by sealed bid unless they are assigned to the fixed assets management function or participating in the establishment of the prices charged in a sales mart environment. This is not to say that the fixed assets management employees do not possess integrity and are not to be trusted. Quite the contrary, it is more a matter of perception and public relations. Regardless of the school of thought advocated, there should be a strictly enforced written policy on the subject.

Distribution Of Proceeds

Since agencies or departments originally expended the funds to purchase the surplus property they are entitled to some return from the sales proceeds. However, at the same time the fixed assets management function has devoted much time in disposing of the assets and also deserves to share in the proceeds of the sale. The determination of the proper share for each is a difficult question especially since we are not normally dealing with a huge amount of money per asset. Some assets, of course, bring a bigger return than others and may involve large sales proceeds. Therefore, a schedule or formula for the division of the funds realized is essential as a policy where each party understands their portion of the proceeds. When large sums are involved there is always more interest in obtaining a share of the proceeds.

Arizona State University uses the following rebate schedule in determining the rebate to a department:[4]

| Surplus Property Sales Rebate Schedule | | | |
| Sales Price | | | |
Greater Than	But Not More Than	Rebate To Department	Of The Amount More Than
$0.00	$100	0%	
$100	$1,000	80%	$100
$1,000	$10,000	$720+90%	$1,000
$10,000	$20,000	$8,820+95%	$10,000
$20,000		$18,320+98%	$20,000

The South Carolina Consolidated Procurement Code states that "The Surplus Property Management Office (SPMO) shall deposit the proceeds from such disposition, less expense of the disposition, in the State's General Fund unless a governmental body makes a written request to retain such proceeds, less cost of disposition, for the purchase of like kind property." Therefore, a South Carolina State agency can make the determination on whether to seek a rebate on the sale of surplus property from their agency. The SPMO has established an administrative fee schedule based on the acquisition cost of the property much like

Arizona State University. The SPMO administrative fee schedule is:

Schedule	Service Charge	Items
A	First $75 of sale proceeds	All vehicles, boats, motors, farm tractors, farm equipment, and other equipment with a unit acquisition coat in excess of $5,000 except as enumerated in Schedule E.
B	First $15 of sale proceeds	Miscellaneous property with a useful life of two or more years at date of purchase and a unit acquisition cost of $5,000 or less. Examples are furniture, office equipment and machines, food service equipment, lawn mowers, and other items not covered under Schedule A.
C	First $15 of sale proceeds	All expendable supplies. Examples are paper, office supplies, hardware, custodial supplies, etc.
D	20% of available sale proceeds plus expenses that are necessary to cover the administrative cost	Confiscated property.

	associated with this program.	
E	2% of first $250,000 of sale proceeds, plus expenses	Special public sales. Items included are airplanes, ships, computer and related high tech equipment, or any item that would necessitate public sale solicitation from a highly specialized market or whose unit acquisition cost exceeds $25,000.

These are but two methods for dealing with the distribution for proceeds for the surplus property sales. Regardless of the method used it seems only fair that agencies or departments receive some form of rebate on the sale of surplus property that they generate. But the return has to take into account the cost of disposition.

Hazardous Materials Handling:

Hazardous waste is byproducts of society that can pose a substantial or potential hazard to human health or the environment when improperly managed, possesses at least one of four characteristics (ignitability, corrosivity, reactivity, or toxicity), or appears on special Environmental Protection Agency (EPA) lists. The National Environmental Policy Act of 1969 was passed to establish a national policy for the environment, to provide for the establishment of a Council on Environmental Quality, and other purposes. The purposes of the Act are: To declare a national policy which will encourage productive and enjoyable harmony between man and his environment; to promote efforts which will prevent or eliminate damage to the environment and biosphere and stimulate the health and welfare of man; to enrich the understanding of the ecological systems and natural resources important to the Nation; and to establish a Council on Environmental Quality.[5] The Reorganization Plan 3 of 1970 established the Environmental Protection Agency (EPA) in the executive branch as an independent agency. The purpose of the EPA is to permit coordinated and effective governmental action to assure the protection of the environment by abating and controlling pollution on a systematic basis. Fixed assets management receives hazardous materials and items containing hazardous materials. It is incumbent upon fixed assets managers to be knowledgeable of the Act and EPA policies and procedures to prevent exposing agency employees and others to hazardous conditions. Other Acts that are of interest to the fixed assets manager are:

Toxic Substances Control Act of 1976: The Act was enacted by Congress to give EPA the ability to track 75,000 industrial chemicals currently produced or imported into the United States. The EPA repeatedly screens these chemicals and can call for reporting or testing of those that may pose an environmental of human-health threat.

Federal Insecticide, Fungicide, and Rodenticide Act of 1972: The primary focus of the Act is to afford federal control of pesticide distribution, sale and use. The EPA was given authority under the Act not only to study the consequences of pesticide usage but also to call for users (farmers, utility companies and others) to register when purchasing pesticides.

Clean Water Act of 1977: The Clean Water Act is an amendment to the Federal Water Pollution Control Act of 1972 which sets the basic structure for regulating discharges of pollutants to waters of the United States. The Act makes it unlawful for any person to discharge any pollutant from a point source into navigable waters unless a permit is obtained under the Act.

Oil Pollution Act of 1990: The Oil Pollution Act streamlined and strengthened EPA's ability to prevent and respond to catastrophic oil spills. The Act requires oil storage facilities and vessels to submit to the Federal government plans detailing how they will respond to large discharges.

Pollution Prevention Act of 1990: The Pollution Prevention Act focused industry, government and public attention on reducing the amount of pollution through cost effective changes in production, operation and raw materials use.

Occupational Safety and Health Act of 1970: Congress passed the Occupational and Safety and Health Act to ensure worker and workplace safety. Their goal was to make sure employers offer their workers a place of employment free from recognized hazards to safety and health, such as exposure to toxic chemicals, excessive noise levels, mechanical dangers, heat or cold stress, or unsanitary conditions.

Public sector agencies come in contact with many hazardous products during the course of operations. Not only should workers be protected but also the environment has to be protected. Non compliance with the various Acts and regulations can result in huge penalties to the agency not to mention the dangers to the workers and environment. Most agencies store or come into contact with hazardous materials and have got to make available for the disposal of the materials whenever they are no longer needed. Additionally, the fixed assets management function may have to store these agents until they can be disposed of properly. Motor pools have used motor oil, brake fluid, antifreeze and transmission fluid that ought to be disposed of properly. In addition, there are common household items that possess hazardous qualities. These items are often turned into property as surplus or excess property. The following are some common household products that possess hazardous qualities, their hazardous properties and disposal method:

Item	Hazard Properties	Disposal Method
Antifreeze	Toxic	Can be recycled. Dispose of through contract with a specialized contractor.
Transmission Fluid	Flammable, toxic	Can be recycled. Dispose of through contract with a specialized contractor.
Brake Fluids	Flammable, toxic	Use up entirely. Empty container can be placed in trash.
Used Oils	Flammable, toxic	Can be recycled. Dispose of through contract with a specialized contractor.
Batteries-Automotive	Corrosive, toxic	Can be recycled at point of purchase.
Toilet Cleaners	Corrosive, toxic, irritant	Use up entirely, empty container can be placed in trash. Save partially full containers to

		dispose of through property function.
Photographic Chemicals	Corrosive, toxic, irritant	Use up entirely, empty container can be placed in trash. Save partially full containers to dispose of through property function.
Disinfectants	Corrosive, toxic	Use up entirely, empty container can be placed in trash. Save partially full containers to dispose of through property function.
Drain Cleaners	Corrosive, toxic	Use up entirely, empty container can be placed in trash. Save partially full containers to dispose of through property function.
Bleach Cleaners	Corrosive, toxic	Use up entirely, empty container can be placed in trash. Save partially full containers to

		dispose of through property function.
Pool Chemicals	Corrosive, toxic	Use up entirely, empty container can be placed in trash. Save partially full containers to dispose of through property function.
Ammonia-Based Cleaners	Corrosive, toxic, irritant	Use up entirely, empty container can be placed in trash.
Abrasive Cleaners or Powders	Corrosive, toxic, irritant	Use up entirely, empty container in trash.
Nickel Cadmium Batteries (found in cellular phones, etc.)	Toxic	Recycle these.
Fungicides	Toxic	Use up entirely, empty container can be placed in trash.
House Plant Insecticide	Toxic	Use up entirely, empty container can be placed in trash.
Herbicides	Toxic	Use up entirely, empty container can be placed in trash.
Enamel or Oil	Flammable, toxic	Use up entirely,

Based Paints		empty container can be placed in trash.
Latex or Water Based Paints	Toxic	Use up entirely, empty container can be placed in trash.
Wood Preservatives	Flammable, toxic	Use up entirely, empty container can be placed in trash.
Stains and Finishes	Flammable, toxic	Use up entirely, empty container can be placed in trash.

Table 4-2: Household Hazardous Waste

Summary

The last step in the Fixed Assets Management Cycle is to surplus or dispose of the property. At this point is the life cycle of the asset it has finally reached the end of its useful life and now has to be disposed of in some manner. The mission of the disposal function is to receive, warehouse and dispose of the agency's surplus property in the best interest of the agency. The central warehousing of surplus property will allow all agency departments one location to acquire needed property which otherwise might escape the system and be sold to the public.

The surplus fixed assets management principles are:

All excess and surplus materials have got to be considered for disposal.

If someone wants it, it has value.

Maximize the sale of surplus property.

Surplus property is defined, as property not needed within the agency. Certain surplus property may begin as surplus property but revolve into another classification. For example, property may be classified as redistribution property if efforts to dispose of it as surplus property have failed. Additionally, excess property may revert to being surplus property and put up for sale if the assets cannot be redistributed within the agency. Surplus property is categorized into five classifications: surplus property, excess property, scrap, redistribution, and recyclable.

After determining that the property is surplus to the needs of the agency, the determination of the best disposal method is necessary. The best method is the one that maximizes the return to the agency or in the case of recyclables the method that returns the materials to use while preserving our natural resources. Careful review and analysis of the items to be disposed of and the determination of the method of disposal is paramount to a successful disposal program. The seven disposal methods are auction, sealed bid, spot sale, trade-in, redistribution, discard, and recycling.

Should employees be allowed to purchase surplus property? There are two schools of thought on the subject. One school of thought is that since the employees are the ones who decide that and when to declare an item to be surplus they should not be allowed to purchase. The other school of thought is that if the items are being disposed of by auction or sealed bid, why disallow them from participating. Each school has its strong points; however, there is not a universal consensus.

Since agencies or departments originally expended the funds to purchase the surplus property and they are entitled to some return from the sales proceeds. However, at the same time the fixed assets management function has devoted much time in disposing of the assets and also deserves to share in the proceeds of the sale. The determination of the proper share for each is a difficult question especially since we are not normally dealing with a huge amount of money per asset. Some assets, of course, bring in a better return than others. Therefore, a formula for the division of the funds realized has to be developed as a policy where each party understands their portion of the proceeds.

Hazardous waste is byproducts of society that can pose a substantial or potential hazard to human health or the environment when improperly managed, possesses at least one of four characteristics (ignitability, corrosivity, reactivity, or toxicity), or appears on special Environmental Protection Agency (EPA) lists. The National Environmental Policy Act of 1969 was passed to establish a national policy for the environment, to provide for the establishment of a Council on Environmental Quality, and other purposes. The purpose of the Act are: To declare a national policy which will encourage productive and enjoyable harmony between man and his environment; to promote efforts which will prevent or eliminate damage to the environment and biosphere and stimulate the health and welfare of man; to enrich the understanding of the ecological systems and natural resources important to the Nation; and to establish a Council on Environmental Quality. The Reorganization Plan 3 of 1970 established the Environmental Protection Agency (EPA) in the executive branch as an independent agency. The purpose of the EPA is to permit coordinated and effective governmental action to assure the protection of the environment by abating and controlling pollution on a systematic basis. Fixed assets management receives hazardous materials and items containing hazardous materials. It is incumbent upon fixed assets managers to be knowledgeable of the Act and EPA policies and procedures to prevent exposing agency employees and others to hazardous conditions.

Questions

1. Describe the surplus property management principles.

2. List the surplus property classifications.

3. Explain the disposal methods.

4. What should sales to employees not be made?

5. Why should the using department be allowed to obtain proceeds from disposal sales?

6. What is hazardous waste?

Notes

[1] *State and Local Government Purchasing, Fourth Edition*, (The national Association of State Purchasing Officials, Lexington, KY, 1994), 101.
[2] *Secondary Markets*,
http://www.dnr.state.oh.us/odnr/recycling/mktdev/secondary.html.
[3] *Paper Recycling An Easy Source Of Extra Income For Anyone*,
wysiwyg://12/http://www.Ungo.net/info-center/business/3416.htm.
[4] *PCS 1001: Equipment Disposal to Surplus Property*,
http://www.asu.edu/aad/manuals/pcs/pcs1001.html.
[5] NEPA, http://es.epa.gov/oeca/ofa/nepa.html.

Chapter 5 Performance Measurements

Purpose

This chapter's purpose is to look at methods to measure and report on the performance of the fixed assets management department.

Objectives

Upon completing this chapter, you should be able to:

- Define performance measurement.

- Briefly describe the fixed assets management performance measurements.

- Use the performance measurement tools to submit reports.

Introduction

One of the purposes of fixed assets management is to secure control over fixed assets. Devices used in the control function are the policies and procedures for safeguarding the agency's assets, the fixed assets records and other information management tools. Controlling is used to illustrate management's attempts to ensure that its policies, procedures and outcomes are in line with its services and financial goals and objectives. Goals and objectives are the backbone for measuring performance. But measuring performance in relation to goals and objectives does not go far enough. There must be a defined system to measure fixed assets management's performance toward meeting its goals and objectives. With goals and objectives in mind, we can use fixed assets management performance measurements to pursue improvement and detect areas that need corrective action.

There is a move for more public scrutiny of government to determine effectiveness, the desire to hold government employees accountable for results rather than stewardship of inputs and nationwide effort to make governments more results-oriented. On the federal side the Government Performance and Results Act of 1993 is the emphasis for federal agencies. The Act required every federal department and agency, by September 30, 1997, to develop a five-year strategic plan linked to measurable outcomes. This linkage was to be preformed via a series of annual performance plans, which was to be required government wide by the beginning of fiscal year 1999.

Advocates of improved performance measurement in local government have long emphasized the importance of suitable performance yardsticks for municipal functions in lieu of the private sector's bottom-line measure of profit or loss. Absent a marketplace barometer of product value and customer satisfaction, well-conceived measures of municipal services would nevertheless offer a gauge of progress or slippage over time-and perhaps even a gauge of performance adequacy relative to targets, standards, or comparison jurisdictions. A scorecard that could provide such information would be as vital to public sector success as it is in any other endeavor where evolving strategies are predicated on the knowledge of whether one is "winning or losing."[1]

One difficulty in measuring fixed assets management's performance is what to measure. There is no well-developed set of performance measures established for fixed assets management, especially in the public sector. The public sector does not operate on the profit motive but on providing service to its customers. Service cannot be measured as effectively as if a profit was being made to use in the measurement formula. Terms such as "good," "bad," "high," or "low" are meaningless without a comparison standard. If there are no measurement standards, it means that

112

performance is not important. Fixed assets management performance is very important to the agency if not the trend must be changed. Upper management must understand the value of fixed assets management and the best way to do that is to use quantitative standards that they understand. A set of performance measurement standards must be developed to show upper management that fixed assets management has a meaningful task and can quantitatively demonstrate it.

Another consideration is why does performance need to be measured. If we are not measuring performance now, why would we want to measure performance. This is the "If it is not broken, don't fix it" syndrome and has no place in the public sector. It is not a matter of fixing something that is not broken. It is a matter of wanting to know how well the fixed assets management function is performing compared to other agency functions and toward the achievement of their goals and objectives. Additionally, performance measurements can be used to provide recognition to those working in fixed assets management. The benefits of performance measurement are:

Strengthens accountability.

Enhances decision-making.

Improves customer service.

Enables agencies to determine effective resource use.

Supports strategic planning and goal setting.

Fairfax County, Virginia summarizes the reasons that performance measurement is essential as:[2]

If you don't measure results, you can't tell success from failure.

If you can't see success, you can't reward it.

If you can't reward success, you're probably rewarding failure.

If you can't see success, you can't learn from it.

If you can't recognize failure, you can't correct it.

If you can demonstrate results, you can win public support.

The tasks of this chapter are to define performance measurement, develop a set of performance measurements and lastly demonstrate how the measurements can be used. Other subjects to be discussed are the tools that can be used to demonstrate performance measurements in a meaningful manner. One must have knowledge and understanding of what performance measurements really are and the importance of applying the measurements. Collecting and analyzing fixed assets management performance is crucial. One of the most difficult tasks will be to establish meaningful and understandable measurements. Once the measurements have been developed they must be presented in a manner that will allow complete understanding of the results. There are certain tools available, such as tables, charts, and graphs that can be used to present the measurements.

What Is Performance Measurement

Fixed assets management performance measurements are the compilation of specific information regarding the results of the fixed assets management function. It includes the measurement of the nature of job that is being accomplished and is considered the basis of managing by results. In the past, most public sector agencies have managed on the basis of inputs such as manpower, budget and volume of workload accomplished. Manpower includes the number of employees to accomplish the fixed assets management tasks and is the most expensive part of any operation. Budget is always expressed in the size of the budget to carry out the job. Budget is measured in dollars and is easy to measure and express quantitatively. It is, also, a measure that is easily understood. Volume is the number of assets tagged or processed, the number of assets disposed of, or it can be expressed in dollars such as the acquisition costs of disposed assets in dollars. These are all input types of measures and do not measure outcome. To manage effectively outcomes must be measured to determine what is actually being accomplished.

Performance measurement is not an end in itself, but is a tool to enable public sector managers to make sound policy and operational decisions. The ability and willingness to monitor and measure the efficiency, effectiveness and quality of fixed assets management programs and services are a mark of good management. Managers need the performance inputs for determining accurate budgets and make strategic plans for the future. They need to know how well the surplus disposal program is doing in a quantitative way. Ratios need to be developed that can express the performance such that long-range plans can be based on facts instead of supposition. If the fixed assets management function is disposing of ten percent of the agency's assets per year, plans can be developed to replace those assets based on quantitative, provable data. The data must be presented on a regularly scheduled basis such that trends can be developed to assist in the planning cycle.

Performance Measurements

The purchasing and inventory control departments have standardized performance measurements that have been developed over the years. Purchasing measures the number of purchase requisitions processed in a given period, the cost to process a purchase order, number of bids processed in a given period and the dollar value of purchases processed. Inventory control measures the number of requisitions processed, stockout rate, inventory turnover rate, and inventory records accuracy. These measurements greatly assist in the day-to-day management of the functions. The purchasing department has been able to implement the use of purchasing cards to purchase many low cost supplies and services because of the high cost to process a purchase order. Performance measurements were used to quantitatively show that the use of the purchasing card could save money for the public sector.

Fixed assets management does not have a well-developed set of performance measurements. However, there are a number of areas that can be successfully measured to show the true performance of the function. The following are measurements that can be made to show the performance of fixed assets management:

Capitalized Assets Owned.

Asset Capitalization Rate.

Disposal Rate.

Redistribution Rate.

Inventory Verification Accuracy Ratio.

The compilations for these performance factors are as follows:

Capitalized Assets Owned: This performance factor indicates the total number of assets managed by the fixed assets management function. It is a very simple measure to compile and express. There are three ways to express this performance factor, first as the number of assets owned, secondly as the total dollar value of all assets owned and thirdly as the average value of all capitalized assets. The value of this performance factor is that it relates the magnitude of the fixed assets management function. Total assets owned will indicate the workload placed on fixed assets management. It also indicates the amount of effort required in the inventory verification program. The more assets owned the greater the physical inventory requirements will be on the departmental custodians.

Capitalized Assets Owned = Total Number of Assets Maintained

Capitalized Assets Owned = 5,234

Value of Capitalized Assets = Total Dollar Value of All Assets Maintained

Value of Capitalized Assets = $33,452,123

Average Value of Capitalized Assets = Total Dollar Value of All Assets Maintained / Total Number of Assets Maintained

Average Value of Capitalized Assets = $33,452,123 / 5,234 = $6,391

Asset Capitalization Rate: The Asset Capitalization Rate is the number and dollar value of assets capitalized over a given period of time. The period should not be less than one month. A final value for the year is a good value to use for comparison with prior years. A review of the measurement will indicate the activity that is taking place within fixed assets management and any seasonal trends. Seasonal trends can be used to justify temporary personnel that may be needed.

Capitalized Assets Added = Total Number of Assets Added For A Given Period (Month and Year)

Capitalized Assets Added = 29 for September

Value of Capitalized Assets Added = Total Dollar Value of All Assets Added For A Given Period (Month and Year)

Value of Capitalized Assets Added = $325,892 for September

Disposal Rate: The Disposal Rate is the number and dollar value of assets being disposed of for a given period of time. There are two disposal rates, one for capitalized assets and one for other assets, each reporting on the number and dollar value of the disposed assets. The dollar value is the acquisition cost of the assets. The dollar rate could be converted to fair market value for a better depiction of the true value of those assets. The period should not be less than a month but will be more effective if reported every three months (a quarter). Additionally, an annual rate should be computed to depict the annual activity. This rate compared to the Capitalized Assets Owned will indicate if capitalized assets are being disposed of faster than they are being replaced.

Capitalized Assets Disposal Rate = Total Number of Disposed Assets For the Quarter

Capitalized Assets Disposal Rate = 22

Other Assets Disposal Rate = 1,234

Value of Capitalized Assets Disposal Rate = Total Dollar Value of All Disposed Assets For the Quarter

Value of Capitalized Assets Disposal Rate = $234, 437

Value of Other Assets Disposal Rate = $8,129

Redistribution Rate: This is the rate of the number and dollar value of excess property redistributed within and external to the agency. This is property that is no longer needed by the custodial department but may be used by another department within the agency or in some cases outside of the agency. This classification includes such items as chairs, desks, vehicles, test equipment office machines, computers, etc. The Redistribution Rate indicates how well the fixed assets management function is meeting it goal and objective of maximizing the reuse of excess property. There should be two rates, one for

118

capitalized assets and one for other property. The period should not be less than a month but will be more effective if reported every three months (a quarter). Additionally, an annual rate should be computed to depict the annual activity for comparison with other years

Capitalized Assets Redistribution Rate = Total Number of Assets Redistributed For the Quarter

Capitalized Assets Redistribution Rate = 35

Other Assets Redistribution Rate = 214

Value of Capitalized Assets Redistribution Rate = Total Dollar Value of All Assets Redistributed For the Quarter

Value of Capitalized Assets Redistribution Rate = $234,785

Value of Other Assets Redistribution Rate = $21,392

Inventory Verification Accuracy Ratio: This rate shows the accuracy of the physical inventory program. It shows the ratio of the number of errors reported during physical inventory. A low ratio shows that the agency fixed assets management program is performing efficiently and effectively. On the other hand a high ratio indicates that there is little control and accountability of agency fixed assets. The ratio is computed by dividing the number of errors reported during inventory by the number if inventories performed. The rate can be shown as an annual rate or as a cyclical rate if the physical inventory is accomplished cyclically.

Inventory Verification Accuracy Ratio = Number of Errors / Number of Verifications X 100

Annual Inventory Verification Accuracy Ratio = 6 / 98 X 100 = 6.1 %

Although the above rates and ratios are but a few that can be used effectively they can be modified to present rates and ratios for subcategories that may be of interest to the agency. The Department of Transportation, for example, may wish to modify the rates to show the rates for heavy equipment owned, disposed of, or redistributed. Rates such as this would assist the department in acquiring addition assets. With the emphasis on high technology it may be that the agency wishes to present the rates for high technology activity. High technology rates will be of interest to education departments and higher education institutions. Effective use of the rates and ratios will greatly assist the fixed assets management function is reporting how well it is performing its mission.

Performance Measurement Tools

Using the rates as portrayed above would make for a very bland report. The rates and ratios by themselves do not maximize their use or lend themselves to presentation. The rates and ratios must be presented to upper management in an understandable form. Upper management does not have the time or inclination to read detailed reports. They are more inclined to scan data and retain the material aspects. Therefore, the presentation of the performance measurements is an important part of the performance measurement process. There are a number of tools that can be used to present the data. Data can be presented in written report format, as a table, or as a graph. All have their advantages and disadvantages.

Written Report Format: The written report is the least desirable type of presentation. This was the preferred type of report during the typewriter era. It is difficult to prepare and is long and boring to read. Use it sparingly.

Fixed Assets Management Monthly Report

The following is the Fixed Assets Management Monthly Report for January 2001.

1. Capitalized Assets Owned:

   Number of Capitalized Assets Owned – 5,234
   Value of Capitalized assets Owned - $33,452, 123
   Average Value of Capitalized Assets - $6,391

2. Asset Capitalization Rate:

   Capitalized Asset Added – 29
   Value of Capitalized Asset Added - $325,892

3. Disposal Rate:

   Capitalized Assets Disposal Rate – 22
   Value of Capitalized Assets Disposal Rate - $234,437

   Other Assets Disposal Rate – 1,234
   Value of Other Assets Disposal Rate - $8,129

4. Redistribution Rate:

   Capitalized Asset Redistribution Rate – 35
   Value of Capitalized Assets Redistribution Rate - $234,785

   Other Assets Redistribution Rate – 214
   Value of Other Assets Redistribution Rate - $21,392

5. Inventory Verification Accuracy Ratio:

   Number of Verifications – 15
   Number of Errors – 2
   Ratio – 13%

   John Jones
   Fixed Assets Manager

Figure 5-1: Written Report

Fixed Assets Management Monthly Report

The following is the Fixed Assets Management Monthly Report for January 2001.

Performance Measure	Rate
Capitalized Assets Owned:	
Assets Owned	5,234
Asset Value	$33,452,123
Average Value	$6,391
Asset Capitalization Rate:	
Assets Added	29
Added Assets Value	$325,892
Disposal Rate:	
Capitalized Assets Disposal Rate	22
Value	$234,437
Other Assets Disposal Rate	1,234
Value	$8,129
Redistribution Rate:	
Capitalized Assets Rate	35
Value	$234,785
Other Assets	214
Value	$21,392
Inventory Verification Accuracy Rare:	
Number of Verifications	15
Number of Errors	2
Ratio	13%

John Jones
Fixed Assets Manager

Figure 5-2: Table Report

Fixed Assets Management
Monthly Report

The following is the Fixed Assets Management Monthly Report for
January 2001.

1. Capitalized Assets Owned:

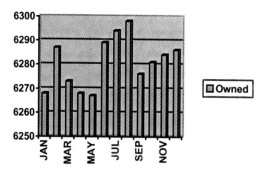

2. Value of Capitalized Assets:

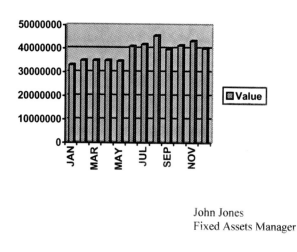

John Jones
Fixed Assets Manager

Figure 5-3: Graph Report

Table Format: Use of a table is a popular presentation method. It allows the data to be presented in a format that is easy to read and scan the data. Tables are easy to create with a word processing package. They can be created with or without grid lines.

Graph Report: Graph reports are the new era. They were very difficult to accomplish prior to the advent of the microcomputer and various application software packages. However, new word processing and specialized graphing packages are available to make the task of creating a graph almost painless. The bar graph is a common graph in use. It can be used to compare the size or magnitude of different figures or one figure over a span of time. The bar graph is used to emphasize the individual amounts or differences in simple, regular data series. The bar graph is well suited for presenting the fixed assets management performance measurements. They are especially well suited for displaying annualized measurements. Figure 5-3 shows the performance measurement Capitalized Assets Owned. The top graph displays the number of assets owned while the bottom graph displays the value of assets owned in dollars. It is readily apparent that although the number of assets has fluctuated over the year the dollar value of the assets has remained rather constant. The data displayed in this manner is easy to interpret and make a comparison something that is appealing to upper management.

Summary

One of the purposes of fixed assets management is to secure control over property. Devices used in the control function are the policies and procedures for safeguarding the agency's assets, the fixed assets records and other information management tools. Controlling is used to illustrate management's attempts to ensure that its policies, procedures and outcomes are in line with its services and financial goals and objectives. Goals and objectives are the backbone for measuring performance. But measuring performance in relation to goals and objectives does not go far enough. There must be a system to measure fixed assets management's performance toward meeting its goals and objectives. With goals and objectives in mind, we can use fixed assets management performance measurements to pursue improvement and detect areas that need corrective action.

One difficulty in measuring fixed assets management's performance is what to measure. There is no well-developed set of performance measures established for fixed assets management, especially in the public sector. The public sector does not operate on the profit motive but on providing service to its customers. Service cannot be measured as effectively as if a profit was being made to use in the measurement formula. Terms such as "good," "bad," "high," or "low" are meaningless without a comparison standard. If there are no measurement standards, it means that performance is not important. Fixed assets management performance is very important to the agency if not the trend must be changed. Upper management must understand what fixed assets management does and the best way to do that is to use quantitative standards that they understand. A set of performance measurement standards must be developed to show upper management that fixed assets management has a meaningful task and can quantitatively demonstrate it. Additionally, performance measurements can be used to provide recognition to those working in fixed assets management. The benefits of performance management are:

Strengthens accountability.

Enhances decision-making.

Improves customer service.

Enables agencies to determine effective resource use.

Supports strategic planning and goal setting.

Fairfax County, Virginia summarizes the reasons that performance measurement is essential as:

If you don't measure results, you can't tell success from failure.

If you can't see success, you can't reward it.

If you can't reward success, you're probably rewarding failure.

If you can't see success, you can't learn from it.

If you can't recognize failure, you can't correct it.

If you can demonstrate results, you can win public support.

In fixed assets management performance measurement is the compilation of specific information regarding the results of the fixed assets management function. It includes the measurement of the nature of job that is being accomplished and is considered the basis of managing by results. In the past, most public sector agencies have managed on the basis of inputs such as manpower, budget and volume of workload accomplished. Manpower includes the number of employees to accomplish the fixed assets management tasks and is the most expensive part of any operation. Budget is always expressed in the size of the budget to carry out the job. Budget is measured in dollars and is easy to measure and express quantitatively. It is, also, a measure that is easily understood. Volume is the number of assets tagged or processed, the number of assets disposed of, or it can be expressed in dollars such as the acquisition costs of disposed assets in dollars. These are all input types of measures and do not measure outcome. To manage effectively outcomes must be measured to determine what is actually being accomplished.

Fixed assets management does not have a well-developed set of performance measurements. However, there are a number of areas that can be successfully measured to show the true performance of the function. The following are measurements that can be made to show the performance of fixed assets management:

Capitalized Assets Owned.

Asset Capitalization Rate.

Disposal Rate.

Redistribution Rate.

Inventory Verification Accuracy Ratio.

Using the rates as portrayed above would make for a very bland report. The rates and ratios by themselves do not maximize their use. The rates and ratios must be presented to upper management in a form that they can understand. Upper management does not have the time or inclination to read detailed reports. They are more inclined to scan data and retain the material aspects. Therefore, the presentation of the performance measurements is an important part of the performance measurement process.

Questions

1. Describe the purpose of performance measurements.

2. List the fixed assets management performance measurements.

3. List the performance measurement tools and the benefit of each.

Notes

[1] David N. Ammons, Public Administration Review, January/February 1995, Vol. 55, No. 1.

[2] *Fairfax County Measures Up*, A Manual for Performance Measurement, Third Edition, (Fairfax County, VA 1999).

Index

A

account number, 67, 72
accountability, 1, 4, 8, 10, 11, 13,
  22, 24, 28,29, 30, 36, 37, 38, 44,
  48, 49, 50, 53, 57, 61, 62, 70,
  71, 72, 73, 84, 88, 113, 119, 125
acquisition, 7, 8, 18, 19, 22, 23,
  31,41, 42, 43, 44, 45, 46, 55, 66,
  67, 69, 72, 76, 77, 94, 99, 199,
  101, 115, 116, 126
acquisition costs, 44, 72, 115, 126
acquisition date, 67, 72
additions, 19, 20, 54
agency name, 66, 119
American Accounting Association,
  11
annual inventory verification, 31
Arizona State University, 99, 100
asset number, 67, 72, 76
auction, 56, 82, 85, 88, 89, 90, 98,
  108
authority, 10, 13, 14, 15, 16, 24, 28,
  29, 30, 31, 34, 38, 43, 48, 57,
  68, 73, 82, 91, 102

B

bar graph, 124
batteries, 96, 104, 106
building, 5, 6, 8, 23, 69

C

capitalization, 7, 8, 28, 31, 43, 44,
  45, 46, 48, 50, 51, 55, 73, 116,
  117, 121, 122
capitalization limit, 8, 43, 44, 45,
  46, 48, 51, 55
cash, 18, 19, 88
centralization, 15, 39, 60
certified checks, 87
charter, 28, 29, 48
Clean Water Act of 1977, 102

Code of Federal Regulations, 3, 9
condition, 36, 41, 46, 57, 67, 77
control, 2, 4, 10, 12, 14, 15, 22, 23,
  28, 29, 30, 31, 32, 33, 34, 35,
  36, 37, 39, 41, 42, 46, 48, 49,
  50, 53, 54, 57, 67, 70, 76, 78,
  102, 111, 115, 119, 124
control and identification, 31, 46,
  54
credit cards, 87,88
custodian, 40, 42, 57, 60, 61, 62,
  72, 75, 76, 77, 78, 117
cyclical inventory verification, 57,
  58, 59, 77

D

dates, 67, 74
decentralization, 15, 16, 39, 60
department,3, 13, 16, 28, 32, 34,
  38, 39, 40, 41, 42, 44, 50, 59,
  60, 61, 62, 63, 69, 72, 74, 75,
  76, 77, 85, 93, 99, 110, 111,
  112, 116, 118, 120
departmentation, 15
depreciation, 9, 11, 12, 68
description, 1, 68, 72, 90
discard, 88, 94, 95, 108
disposal methods, 80, 83, 85, 86,
  88, 89, 94, 108, 110
disposal rate, 116, 118, 121, 122,
  127
distribution of proceeds, 80, 98
donated assets, 31, 45

E

Environmental Protection Agency,
  101, 102, 109
equipment, 2, 4, 5, 6, 7, 9, 15, 19,
  22, 40, 41, 44, 48, 50, 53, 69,
  82, 85, 88, 91, 94, 100, 101,
  118, 120
equipment management, 2
etching, 47, 55
exception principle, 14, 33

CPSIA information can be obtained at www.ICGtesting.com
Printed in the USA
LVOW10s1336051014

407334LV00001B/59/A